Praise for *From No-Knead to Sourdough*

Victoria writes with a fine blend of passion and common sense, with informative asides like "Sexy Science Talk." There are few things more soul-satisfying than the taste of homemade sourdough, and even fewer things as healthful to keep your mind and body tuned and balanced. Victoria's detailed but uncluttered recipes make that argument, delectably.

— STEPHEN YAFA, author, *Grain of Truth: Why Eating Wheat Can Improve Your Health*

Victoria Miller cleverly combines science, history, and personal touches to make homemade bread accessible for everyone, no matter his or her level of experience. I've made my own bread for years, and I find this book helpful, friendly, and inspiring. Miller's experiences homesteading and scratch cooking combine with bread-making instruction to bring a connectivity between baking and living off of the land that is refreshing and holistic.

— MEREDITH LEIGH, author, *The Ethical Meat Handbook* and *Pure Charcuterie*

I think baking is a lot like gardening: it's as old as the hills, but we're still experimenting and still learning. That's a good thing, especially given our interest in learning to create handmade bread. And as usual, reading Victoria's writing is a pleasure in and of itself.

— GEORGE and JOLIE WILL, home bread bakers

Victoria Miller brings the art and science of breadmaking to life in her newest book that is surely destined to be a family favorite. Her no-nonsense style cuts through the controversy of gluten vs gluten-free, and along with gluten-free options provides a balanced approach to this hot topic. If you are seeking a new hobby that the whole family will love, look no further than *From No Knead to Sourdough.*

— HANNAH CRUM, co-author, *The Big Book of Kombucha*

Eclectic homesteader Victoria Redhed Miller takes us on a journey that's part science, part art and part passion, infused with a lot of history and can-do! *From No-Knead to Sourdough* is a fresh approach to bringing the joys of bread making into virtually any kitchen setting and has plenty to feed both experienced bakers and neophytes.

— HANK WILL, Editorial Director, Ogden Publications

From No-Knead to Sourdough is destined to have a permanent place among my favorite cookbooks! Enough craft for my inner artist, enough science for my inner nerd, this book cuts through the mystery of bread baking with easy-to-follow recipes and instructions that will get you into your groove in no time. I no longer fear bagels, and sourdough is next on my list!

— CALLENE RAPP, co-author, *Raising Rabbits for Meat*, and owner, The Rare Hare Barn, LLC

Kneaded into the spirit of this profoundly useful book is a deeper message reminding us that bread is a spiritual staple in human society. Victoria Redhed Miller brings the delicious and wholesome essence of homemade bread back into our lives in a straightforward and practical way. At the same time she enriches our spirit with a new awareness of good bread's elevating presence in our lives, like the aroma of a new loaf wafting from the oven. Thank you, Victoria!

— BRYAN WELCH, former publisher, *Mother Earth News, Mother Earth Living* and
Utne Reader; and author, *Beautiful & Abundant: Building the World We Want*

If you're like me, and bread baking and working with dough is out of your comfort zone, this book will take you step-by-step through the learning curve, and your home kitchen will transform into your dream bakery. *From No-Knead to Sourdough* is so much more than another bread baking book; this one comes complete with a supportive friend in the kitchen! Victoria methodically makes bread baking so simple and accessible that you too will share her enthusiasm and expertise. I have to run. I have another loaf needing to come out of the oven.

— LISA KIVIRIST, author, *Soil Sisters: A Toolkit for Women Farmers* and *Homemade for Sale*

Victoria Redhed Miller's clear instructions and the well-organized structure of this book allow for experienced bakers to jump right to recipes, and provide beginners with thorough (but not overwhelming) descriptions of processes. What I particularly like is how she brings bread baking down to the real world. Informative, useful, and entertaining. What more could you want in a book?

— JEREME ZIMMERMAN, author of *Brew Beer Like a Yeti* and *Make Mead Like a Viking*

From No-Knead to Sourdough is an essential volume for anyone aspiring to a regenerative lifestyle and to live more healthfully and self-sufficiently. Victoria guides readers of all experience levels through the joys and intricacies of bread-making by offering a graceful balance of easy to follow steps and deeper science.

— OLIVER GOSHEY, Abundant Edge

If you follow the guidelines in this book, I guarantee you too will produce appealing, tasty, nutritious breads, all in the comfort of your own kitchen and within your COMFORT ZONE! Victoria has done the research and the testing for you, ready for you to learn and master the art of handmade bread making.

— COLLEEN LAMB, M.Ed., owner, Dungeness River Lamb Farm and Lamb Farm Kitchen

FROM NO-KNEAD TO SOURDOUGH

A SIMPLER APPROACH TO
HANDMADE BREAD

VICTORIA REDHED MILLER

new society
PUBLISHERS

Cover design by Diane McIntosh. Cover image ©iStock (626536198).
Interior images: ©setory; ©green2; ©pilarts; ©ananaline;
p 1, 59 ©volff; p 99 ©WavebreakMediaMicro; p 127, 159 ©StockPhotoPro;
p 181 ©valuzza15/Adobe Stock.

Printed in Canada. First printing April 2018.

Inquiries regarding requests to reprint all or part of *From No-Knead to Sourdough*
should be addressed to New Society Publishers at the address below.
To order directly from the publishers, please call toll-free (North America)
1-800-567-6772, or order online at www.newsociety.com

Any other inquiries can be directed by mail to

New Society Publishers
P.O. Box 189, Gabriola Island, BC V0R 1X0, Canada
(250) 247-9737

Library and Archives Canada Cataloguing in Publication

Miller, Victoria Redhed, author
From no-knead to sourdough : a simpler approach to handmade bread
/ Victoria Redhed Miller.

Includes index.
Issued in print and electronic formats.
ISBN 978-0-86571-883-8 (softcover).—ISBN 978-1-55092-676-7 (PDF).—
ISBN 978-1-77142-271-0 (EPUB)

1. Bread. 2. Dough. 3. Baking. 4. Cookbooks. I. Title.

TX769.M55 2018   641.81′5   C2018-901876-3
                                                        C2018-901877-1

Funded by the Government of Canada | Financé par le gouvernement du Canada

New Society Publishers' mission is to publish books that contribute
in fundamental ways to building an ecologically sustainable and just society,
and to do so with the least possible impact on the environment,
in a manner that models this vision.

For my mother,
Sue Redhed,
my first, best teacher.

I'll always be grateful for your lifelong example
of the dignity and joy of being a homemaker;
turns out, it involves a lot more than
building chicken coops.

Thanks, Mum.

Contents

Foreword

by J. Lauryl Jennings

I failed chemistry in high school. The stringent application of math, chemicals, measurements, and heat just didn't sit well with my adventurous, fly-by-the-seat-of-my-pants nature. I've always looked at rules to be more like guidelines, something that is more for interpretation (or desecration) than implementation. That personality trait makes for interesting fiction writing but terrible chemistry—and baking is all about the chemistry.

That fact was not lost on me when my dear friend, Victoria Redhed Miller, asked me to test sourdough recipes for this book. I felt like I was going to fail chemistry class all over again and relive the pain of explaining to my father why I didn't have a Nobel Prize to my name yet. And although Victoria assured me that she had a foolproof process for this super mysterious scientific method of making sourdough, I knew I was a most amazing fool. Fortunately, helping my friend was far more important than looking idiotic, so I rolled up my sleeves and worked the recipes she gave me…and I made some of the best-tasting sourdough I'd ever eaten, in spite of myself.

I was shocked. If my chemistry textbook had read like this fine volume in your hands, I might have gone on to a career in science and created something incredible like organic plastic that tastes like kiwifruit. (At the very least, I'd have passed chemistry with flying colors.) Victoria idiot-proofed the process of making sourdough bread and turned its esoteric mysteries into factual, accomplishable reality. This meant that almost any creature with an opposable thumb could make fermented bread. Even me.

The tool set you'll find within these pages does contain some rules, mind you, but along with those rules are the "hows" and "whys" of why you should follow them, along with a smattering of options about how you can get creative in the margins, and really expand your repertoire in baked goods. There are no restrictions, no limits to the usefulness of *From No-Knead to Sourdough*; the information here will serve you from your first loaf beginnings to the day you open a crumpet café— and beyond.

May your journey into the bread world be a creative one,

— J. Lauryl Jennings
Author of *Apart*

J. Lauryl Jennings is the lightly known author of *Apart*. She's usually scribbling fancy words when shes not practicing hypnotherapy, massage, or baking no-knead sourdough bread.

Introduction: Pure Bread

With bread and wine, you can walk your road.
— SPANISH PROVERB

When my second book, *Craft Distilling*, was published in January 2016, I was asked, "How did you go from writing a book about poultry (*Pure Poultry*, New Society Publishers, 2013) to writing a book about distilling?" I responded with the first thing that came to my mind: "When you read my third book, you'll see the connection."

I didn't even know, at the time, what my third book would be.

Now that I do know what my book is, the connection is clear: It's all about my love of traditional homesteading skills. Raising poultry for meat and eggs; brewing and distilling; using a hand-built, wood-fired oven for baking, cooking, and other homestead chores...to me these are all symbolic of the kind of life my pioneer predecessors lived and the kind of life I myself have dreamed of living.

My husband's grandparents bought this off-grid homestead back in the 1930s. There is a lot of family history here, and, long before I met him, David had daydreams of his own about living here someday. When we moved to the homestead in 2006, we were making a huge transition from big-city life to something very different. I was amazed at how quickly I got past my initial apprehensions and began to see how my love of learning, mechanical skills, and problem-solver personality fit perfectly with the more physical, outdoorsy, hands-on kind of life we had chosen to pursue.

So how do these relate to each other? I am continually fascinated by the way seemingly dissimilar activities actually tie together in a natural, pleasing way. For example, hand-kneading bread dough mimics the process of blending clay and sand into cob to build my outdoor oven. Our chickens, turkeys, and ducks love to eat the mashed grains left over from brewing and distilling processes, and their manure strengthens the natural plaster that I used to finish my oven and give it some weather resistance. That oven is used not only to cook and bake; as it cools, it becomes the perfect place to dry the wood that will fuel the next day's fire. And the sourdough bread baked in that oven is the product of natural fermentation processes exactly like those involved in making beer and wine, yogurt and cheese, pickles, sauerkraut, and kombucha.

From No-knead to Sourdough is a tangible manifestation of one of the true passions of my life: baking bread. Like most people, I started out making simple yeast breads. Years later, I discovered an interest in naturally leavened, or sourdough, bread. This is *pure* bread, bread at its most basic, bread that relies on native wild yeast to raise it and to create its unique flavor, through the magic of fermentation.

Like the craft of distilling, creating bread involves various scientific processes. For more experienced bakers, or bakers interested in the science of fermentation and baking, I include those details in sidebars; for those who simply prefer to learn to make a variety of yeast or sourdough breads without learning all of the whys and wherefores, the text provides clear, user-friendly guidance. My main goal is to minimize the intimidation factor that seems inherent in the process of bread baking. In addition, I aim to challenge the notion that all bread is somehow bad for us.

You don't need to do things the way I do. In fact, I encourage you to pick a place to start, get comfortable with the basics, and then let your imagination and creativity take over as you push the boundaries of your initial comfort zone. Bread baking allows an enormous amount of flexibility to experiment—what I like to think of as the art and craft of baking. Not everyone has the opportunity, the space, or the inclination to build a wood-fired oven, but everyone *can* find ways to move toward self-reliance, energy independence, and a simpler, more meaningful life. Isn't that what we all want?

We all have to eat, and there is no more historically important, elementally satisfying, easily accessible food to make than bread. So many of our memories are connected with food; it makes me incredibly happy to think of you—yes, *you*—beginning to create your own memories as you learn to make your own handcrafted bread.

Daydream. Dream *big*. Be fearless in taking that first step, and believe you can do it. You *can*, you know. Enjoy the journey—and the bread.

PART ONE

FINDING YOUR COMFORT ZONE

Handmade Bread:
It's No Wonder

*How can a nation be called great
when its bread tastes like Kleenex?*
— Julia Child

I WAS FORTUNATE ENOUGH to grow up with a mother who cooked nearly everything from scratch. In addition to cooking meals and packing lunches for our large family, she began baking bread when I was young. She typically made four loaves at a time, three times a week, to meet the toast, garlic bread, and sandwich needs of the ten of us. One of my favorite memories of those years was Mum timing the bread so it was coming out of the oven just when we were getting home from school—a particularly wonderful, welcoming, warming smell on those cold, wet Northwest winter days.

My mother mixed up her bread dough in a contraption I remember as simply "the bread-maker." It was a heavy dough hook with a wooden handle, connected to a lid that clamped onto the rim of a large, deep pot. The pot sat in a simple base with suction cups that held it securely in place on the counter. She put the ingredients in the pot, clamped on the lid, and cranked the handle. The dough hook sat just above the bottom of the pot, so it mixed the ingredients quite thoroughly and efficiently without scraping the sides or bottom of the pot. I don't re-member how long she had to crank, but once the mixing was done, she simply left the dough in the covered pan to rise. Later, she removed it,

FIGURE 1.1. Mum's "bread-maker."

shaped it, and put it into bread pans to rise a second time before baking.

Nowadays, bread bakers are advised to let loaves cool for at least an hour before cutting; cutting bread while it's hot, we are told, releases moisture from the bread as steam, resulting in bread with a shorter shelf life. But on baking day, trudging home hungrily from school and opening the front door to that familiar-yet-indescribable aroma, who could wait for it to cool? Of course, when bread is hot, you really can't slice it thinly. So, crowding around the kitchen island and the cooling racks full of golden-brown loaves, we would wait impatiently for Mum to carve off thick slabs for each of us. We slathered the hot, moist bread with butter and homemade raspberry jam, oh boy!

Clearly, shelf life was not much of an issue when it came to Mum's homemade bread.

From Hand-cranked to Sourdough

I began cooking at a fairly young age; my first memory of cooking is of making beef stew when I was about six years old. Mum always encouraged my siblings and me in whatever hobbies we took an interest in, and at the time, other than music and reading, cooking was my main extra-curricular source of enjoyment. I'm not sure exactly when my interest in bread was first sparked, but it was likely around the time Mum was learning to bake bread. I remember hovering nearby, waiting my turn to take a few cranks at the dough, and probably I was asking endless questions at the time. I'm sure I was baking things like cookies long before ever trying my hand at bread, which at the time seemed complicated and rather mysterious.

Remember all those wonderful Time-Life books that were popular back in the 1970s and 1980s? You would sign up for the series; they would send one book about every other month, which you just paid for as you went along. In junior high, I wanted to be a marine biologist, and one Time-Life series we had was *The Undersea World of Jacques Cousteau*. Oh how I would devour each volume as it arrived, and how I looked forward with junior-high impatience to the arrival of the next! I got certified as a scuba diver when I was in 9th grade, and I have no doubt I was inspired by reading about Cousteau and his adventures in those books.

One of my very favorite Time-Life book sets was *The Family Creative Workshop* (FCW), about 24 volumes, organized alphabetically like an encyclopedia. It was mainly article after article about an enormous variety of handicrafts: We learned crafts like quilling, macramé, soft sculpture, candle-making…

FIGURE 1.2. The beloved *Family Creative Workshop* book series.

I even learned to do calligraphy, a skill that remains to this day. (My twin sister and I were always trying new things we learned from these books, to the point where the family joke was "Vicki and Lindy and their Craft-of-the-Week.") The FCW series also had many articles about food, and I'm sure my initial interest in making cheese and beer came from those volumes. Because the subjects were listed alphabetically, I had read through quite a few volumes before discovering the topic of…*sourdough bread*.

At that point, I had never made bread myself, although I had an idea of the process from all those hours looking over Mum's shoulder as she mixed, kneaded, punched down, shaped, proofed, and baked loaves. I do remember being absolutely fascinated reading about sourdough. How the Forty-Niners would carry a small amount of starter with them, to enable them to make flapjacks and bannock out in the northern wilderness, sustaining them when their search for gold took them far from the nearest trading posts. How sourdough bread developed a unique flavor, and even the crust was somehow different. The method relied entirely on wild yeast, supplied by a culture that you could

FIGURE 1.3. The bread article in the *Family Creative Workshop* book that ignited my interest in bread.

easily make yourself if you planned ahead. The photo of a crusty, beautiful sourdough baguette just out of the oven fascinated me.

(Incidentally, I still have the entire set of *The Family Creative Workshop* books. I liberated it from the Goodwill pile when my parents were downsizing, moving from their home of 31 years in 2003. I still use it, too!)

In 1999, my father retired from his job as a computer programmer and systems analyst at Boeing. That same year, he was diagnosed with Type 2 diabetes. My father, as was typical for him, asked lots of questions, wanted to understand what was happening, and was quite disciplined about the inevitable changes to his diet. I remember him saying that his doctor told him he could eat sourdough but not other bread. Why, I wondered, was sourdough so different that a diabetic was allowed to eat it? I don't remember asking questions about it at the time, but I'm quite sure that this was the first time I began to be seriously interested in sourdough. I didn't actively pursue it then. But the seed was planted somewhere in the back of my mind.

Over the years, I grew to love baking of all kinds, but for as far back as I can remember, I have particularly loved to bake bread. Is it the soothing rhythm of hand-kneading, feeling the loose, wet ingredients come together in a smooth, supple, springy dough? The apparently magical influence of unseen yet very active tiny yeast cells in contact with grain and water? The yeasty, tangy smell and the way fully developed dough feels in my hands as I coax it into its final shape? Or is it merely that tantalizing, comforting aroma that fills the house as bread bakes and elicits the same comment every time from my husband when he walks into the house: "Wow, something sure smells great in here!"

Whatever the reasons, I simply love baking bread. I *love* it.

My husband, David, an avid bread baker himself for many years, had had an outdoor bread oven on his wish list since long before I met him. Several years after we moved to our off-grid homestead in 2006, David was buying locally made "artisan" bread at a nearby store. Even back then, it generally cost $5 to $6 per loaf. It was good bread, but the problem was it didn't stay fresh for long, and David has strong feelings about bread being fresh. With just the two of us at home, we would usually be barely halfway through the loaf before it was stale enough that he wouldn't eat it. Not wanting to waste it, I would usually keep eating it until it was basically too hard to cut, and even then, some usually went uneaten. That was about the time I decided, after a few years of not baking much at all, to go back to making bread. This time, I took the plunge and determined to try my hand at "real" sourdough bread.

Thinking Outside the Breadbox

I must say, I was a bit intimidated by the process. I like to research thoroughly before I try something new, and sourdough bread was no exception. I soon found that there is a lot of conflicting and confusing information about sourdough. A book I recently read described the idea of relying on wild yeasts as unpredictable at best, complicated, best left to the professionals, and more likely to fail than to succeed. Some sources said you must measure ingredients for the starter precisely, monitor it closely for days and "feed" it up to four times a day. Other sources said to "refresh" or "feed" the starter at least once a week. One book suggested fermenting the dough (whatever that meant) at a relatively cool temperature, while another recommended warmer temperatures. Eventually, about the time my eyes were glazing over for the umpteenth time, I followed my usual course of action when learning a new skill: I put the books down, picked a day and time to start, and began the process of cultivating my first sourdough starter.

At the time, I had very little idea of where that decision would lead me. I had only minimal understanding, when I began, of what sourdough was, how to work with it, and why making bread with it makes such a difference compared to baking with commercial yeast. When I was growing up, we didn't watch a lot of television, but I can remember commercials for Wonder Bread: "Helps build strong bodies 12 ways!" the voice-over trumpeted. The language impressed me as a youngster; who didn't want a strong body? When I began seriously studying bread in general and sourdough in particular, I learned that the "12" in those ads referred to vitamins and minerals that were put back *into* the bread, because it was made with flour so highly processed as to retain very little of the original nutrients of the grain.

In 1850, most of the United States was still rural, a land of pioneers and homesteads. Back then, at least 90% of all bread consumed in America was homemade. Wonder Bread was introduced by Continental Baking in 1927, during an era of huge transition for homemakers. Vacuum cleaners, washing machines, electric cookers—all kinds of labor-saving devices flooded the market, a dazzling vista for frazzled wives and mothers. The prospect of being able to buy soft, cheap white bread that kids loved must have been irresistible. Then, in 1930, the vista became even rosier with the introduction of pre-sliced bread.

From Big City to off the Grid

For reasons I've never quite understood (having lived the first 45 years of my life in Seattle), I have, since I was young, always felt more at home in small towns. I was always drawn to traditional skills and crafts, always loved the idea of learning a trade or skill by means of an apprenticeship to a master and passing that on to someone else. Always leaned toward "old-fashioned" values, a simple life of hard work, outdoor chores, and hands-on learning, building, repairing, and restoring. So I suppose it's no big surprise that in a world of kitchen machines and gadgets, I am so enamored of the process of making bread with a few simple ingredients, mixing and kneading dough by hand, fermenting it in a cool corner of my kitchen, then baking it in the high heat of a hand-built, wood-fired oven.

For me, making any kind of bread, in any kind of oven, is a deeply satisfying experience that never wears thin. My baking life continues to include simple no-knead yeast breads, as well as those made with a pre-ferment like the Italian ciabatta. Still, having eventually pushed my way through my initial comfort zone, I discovered the seemingly unlimited variety of sourdough breads. Using the same starter culture I have maintained since 2010, kneading the dough by hand, and baking it the same way my pioneer ancestors did...well, let's put it this way: If I were a cat, I would be purring with contentment. It is absolutely a labor of love. And it's no Wonder.

Getting in the Zone:
How to Use This Book

*I'd rather teach you how to make bread
than give you a slice of my bread.*
— Genereux Philip

Originally this book was going to be all about sourdough breads. In recent months, having done quite a few presentations on this subject at events like the Mother Earth News Fair, I realized I had been using too narrow a lens to view this project. I discussed it with my editor, reworked the table of contents, and this is the result: a book that allows, no, *encourages* you to find your own comfort zone with bread, as opposed to a book that tries to convince you that sourdough is for everyone.

Participants ask a lot of questions at these presentations, and I pay attention to them. About the fourth time around, I noticed some questions were being asked over and over: Can I make sourdough using the no-knead method? Is it possible to make a gluten-free sourdough starter? Isn't sourdough starter complicated and time-consuming to maintain? The light-bulb moment for me was hearing that people really are interested in making their own bread, but they are often intimidated by conflicting information and concerns about fitting it into their schedules. That's when I first realized that my original concept didn't consider the needs of new or relatively inexperienced bakers.

I am so grateful for the opportunity to have had this kind of feedback long before this book was written. I'm convinced that this incarnation is a much better book, and I'm confident that regardless of your current level of baking experience, you will find something here to dive into quite fearlessly. Making your own bread isn't difficult, and it should be fun!

So, how do you use this book? Well, first there are a few chapters covering the basics: equipment, ingredients, how to mix, knead, ferment, shape, and bake bread; there's even a whole chapter on the subject of gluten! From there, it's organized into several different comfort zones, beginning with no-knead breads. If you've never baked bread before, I suggest you start here. When you feel ready, I encourage you to move on to the next comfort zone. At any point, if you're happy with the results and are having fun, there's no need to leave that comfort zone. It's always up to you. I do think you'll find, though, that once you have been thoroughly bitten by the baking bug, you're likely to have the confidence, and the interest, to try something new.

Whatever your comfort zone, I highly recommend that you read the chapters leading up to Comfort Zone 1 (Chapter 8). If you're a more experienced baker and prefer to go straight to the recipes, see the recipe index at the back of the book. Or, if you've made yeast bread before but want to try your hand at sourdough, skip ahead to that comfort zone. There are interesting recipes to try in every section, though, so I hope you'll read through the whole thing; you might be surprised at what you can learn!

Sexy Science Talk

There is a lot of science to the art of bread-baking, and it's helpful to understand at least a little to give some context to what I'll be teaching you to do. I find it all quite fascinating, and I spent hours on interesting but fairly frivolous tangents while researching, and learned a heck of a lot. But don't worry, I'm not going to whack you over the head with all those fascinating details. In trying to make this book user friendly, I decided to include a certain amount of the science, but separately in sidebars. This way, those of you who care about such issues can read all about it, and others who only want to get on with making bread can stay with the main text and get thoroughly grounded in just what you need to know to get started.

When texting with my novelist friend J. Lauryl (Jenn) Jennings one day, I was expounding on the riveting subject of yeast hydrolysis (I know, I know), and Jenn, being the angelically patient and supportive friend that she is, texted back: "Ooh, sexy science talk!" Naturally I latched right onto that phrase, and the science-y sidebars are headed Sexy Science Talk. I have tried to make even the science stuff clear, relevant, and even a little fun, so don't be surprised if you find yourself reading them unintentionally.

Handmade Bread Ain't Perfect

The photos in this book are all of bread I have made myself, either in my kitchen oven or my outdoor wood-fired oven. Any time you make something by hand, such as bread, there will be variations in the results. I've seen too many cookbooks that have beautiful studio photography; unfortunately when I follow a recipe and my results don't resemble the one in the cookbook photo, I feel like I've messed up somehow. The truth is, even with all my experience, I can make the same bread recipe ten times in a row and get slightly different results each time. Why? Maybe the fermenting temperature was a little cooler or warmer, possibly I got distracted and the dough proofed a little longer than usual, or I was sloppy with my shaping technique; whatever the reason, it just won't always look "perfect." I prefer to give you a realistic idea of what to expect, so you're not going to see a lot of perfect bread here.

Take Your Time and Have Fun!

I know how fortunate I am to have learned to bake from my mother. If you have a friend, neighbor, mother, or grandma who's willing to share advice and experience, it can be a big help. If you are new to baking bread, it will seem like a steep learning curve at first. Do try to give yourself plenty of time, be easy on yourself, and keep at it. Before long you'll notice that you aren't referring to the book as often, movements like kneading and shaping are becoming almost automatic, and the results will be more consistent. I promise you, the joy of taking a few simple ingredients and turning them into something delicious, beautiful, and nutritious is something you can be very proud to accomplish. When you find yourself looking forward with anticipation to baking day, you'll know you've found your comfort zone. Way to go, you!

Flour, Salt, Yeast, Water

What makes good bread?
It is a question of good flour and slow fermentation.
— John Hillaby

THERE ARE MANY good sources of information on different flours. There are also many choices; just selecting a plain old wheat bread flour can be positively mind-boggling. I've kept track of the questions I get most often at presentations and on my website, and compiled all my research and experience into a fairly compact discussion below. It includes a few notes on the differences between American flour and European flour, the subject of frequent conversations these days.

This chapter covers gluten grains and a few basic bread-baking ingredients; non-gluten grains will be discussed in Chapter 4.

Flours

I don't specifically recommend one brand of flour over another. I do suggest you buy the freshest flour you can find, locally milled if possible, from a vendor whose inventory turns over regularly.

If it's available in your area, I recommend using stone-ground or stone-milled flour. The advantage of stone milling is the cooler temperature generated in the process, resulting in less nutrient loss. When I can find stone-ground white flour, I buy it, albeit in smaller than usual quantities; it is more perishable because a little of the germ oil remains

FIGURE 3.1. A few of the many choices in bread flours.

in the flour. However, stone-ground white flour is more nutritious because it absorbs some of the nutrients from the bran and the germ before they are sifted out. Roller-milled flour loses more of these nutrients because the bran and the germ are removed so early in the milling process.

When buying whole wheat flour, especially, try to avoid the bags on grocery store shelves; if possible, find whole wheat flour that has been refrigerated. This recommendation applies to *all* whole-grain flour, including whole-grain gluten-free flours.

Here are a few other factors to consider when buying flour, especially wheat flours.

Organic or Non-organic?

There is no definitive evidence that organic flour performs better in baking. To me, the advantage of using organic grains is avoiding ingredients like bromates and other bleaching agents. I'm not convinced there is any discernible difference in taste or baking performance between organic and non-organic flours. However, I do recommend using organic grains when you're activating a new sourdough starter (see Chapter 16); otherwise, the choice is largely a matter of preference or availability.

Bleached or Unbleached?

Bleaching is a method of oxidizing wheat proteins. Passive oxidation occurs during storage; commercially, flours are stored 3 to 8 weeks before being sold. Why is flour bleached? Aging or oxidizing agents can increase the end-to-end linking of glutenin molecules and thus increase dough strength.

Bleaching and bromate are *not* allowed in Europe; other differences between American flours and European flours are discussed below.

High-production commercial mills speed up the oxidation process by bleaching the flour; chlorine gas, and then potassium bromate, are used to artificially oxidize flour. In the late 1980s, American millers, concerned about the reported toxicity of bromate, began replacing it with ascorbic acid. (Ascorbic acid, or vitamin C, is actually an *anti*-oxidant, but it becomes oxidized to dehydroascorbic acid, which in turn oxidizes gluten proteins.)

As with so many foods these days, you need to read the labels. Be aware that white flour labeled "unchlorinated" may have other bleaching or oxidizing agents; to be on the safe side, look for certified organic flour, or unbleached, unbromated flour.

I would definitely avoid using bleached flour for making sourdough starters and bread, because bleaching chemicals may affect the growth and balance of yeast and bacterial populations. You're trying to feed your yeast and lactobacilli, not starve them into submission.

What About Grinding Your Own Flour?

Here's what you need to know: Fresh flour is harder to work with than aged flour. Freshly ground flour tends to produce a dough that is too springy and elastic to knead and shape easily. It forms a weak gluten network and a slack dough, so it is also reluctant to rise, resulting in a dense baked loaf.

Oxidation of the flour helps because oxygen in the air gradually frees the glutenin proteins' end sulfur groups to react with each other and form the longer gluten chains that increase the elasticity of the dough.

This disadvantage is most apparent when working with wheat, since wheat has by far the most gluten of all the grains. If you want to grind your own wheat, you should do that. I simply suggest you don't use that flour right away, if you're using it to make bread, especially fast-rising yeast bread.

Decisions, Decisions...

There's a lot to think about when choosing flour. Ultimately, of course, the choice is up to you. Let's take a look at the most common types of flour you're likely to buy for baking, starting with the gluten grains: wheat, rye, and barley. (Non-gluten grains are discussed in Chapter 4.)

Wheat

American wheat varieties fall into these categories: hard or soft; winter or spring; and red or white.

* **Hard wheat** has high protein and more gluten, making it ideal for bread.
* **Hard wheat** has more gluten than soft wheat.
* **Soft wheat** tends to have richer flavor than hard wheat.
* **Winter wheat** is generally higher in minerals.
* **Spring wheat** has more gluten than winter wheat, even if it's the same variety.
* **Hard red winter wheat** has moderate protein content, good for bread, rolls, and all-purpose flour.
* **Hard red spring wheat** has the highest protein of all the bread wheats.
* **Soft red winter wheat** has low protein, good for cakes, pastries, crackers.
* **Hard white winter wheat** is similar to hard red winter wheat but lacks the pigmentation of red wheat.
* **Durum wheat** is very hard, high-protein wheat, used to make semolina flour for pasta.
* **All-purpose flour** is a blend of soft and hard wheats; the actual

content varies widely. In most of the US and Canada, all-purpose flour has more protein than all-purpose flour in southern states and the northwest.

* **Flour** labeled "bread flour" is usually 12% to 13% protein and is either hard winter or hard spring wheat.

Other types of wheat

* **Emmer**, also known as farro in Italy, is a tetraploid wheat (see Sexy Science Talk) used mainly for bread and, in Italy, as a whole grain in soup. It is higher in fiber than other wheats.
* **Kamut** (Egyptian for wheat) is a registered trademark for an ancient relative of durum wheat. Kamut has high protein, but its gluten is better suited for making pasta than bread.
* **Spelt** is a high-protein (up to 17%) wheat. Some people who are sensitive to gluten can tolerate the lower levels of gluten in spelt.
* **Triticale**, a cross between wheat and rye, is mostly grown for use as animal feed. The bread-making qualities of most types are not as good as wheat.

> ### SEXY SCIENCE TALK
>
> ## The Genetics of Wheat
>
> The three groups of wheat varieties according to number of chromosomes: Einkorn is diploid (2 sets of 7); emmer (i.e., durum) is tetraploid (4 sets of 7); bread wheat, spelt, and club wheat are hexaploid (6 sets of 7); this group accounts for 90% of US wheat production. Most of the remainder is durum wheat. Club wheat is used for pastry and cake flour.
>
> Einkorn reportedly has less sugar-spiking amylopectin starch and more slow-releasing amylase than other types of wheat.

Rye

Rye is a gluten grain, but compared with wheat, it has very little gluten, and rye's ratio of soluble to insoluble proteins is not optimal for gluten formation. Its gas-trapping ability mainly comes from the presence of pentosans, chains of sugars structurally similar to starches and cellulose. Rye also has about 50% more fat than wheat.

Pentosans are hygroscopic (water-loving), so they help rye breads stay moist and fresh longer. Rye pentosans also help control appetite. Rye absorbs 8 times its weight in water, compared with wheat, which absorbs twice its weight in water. If you've ever wondered why you feel so full after eating rye crackers, now you know: dried carbohydrates in rye crackers absorb liquid and swell in the stomach, giving a sensation of fullness, and are slowly and only partially digested.

The labeling of rye flour is often confusing and inconsistent. Most commercial rye is roller milled and is generally not a whole-grain product. *White rye* is from the center of the endosperm. *Cream* or *light rye* includes the next layer of endosperm; *dark rye* includes the outside of the endosperm. *Rye meal* is coarser, ground from the whole kernel. An even coarser grade of rye meal is often called *pumpernickel*.

Barley contains significant quantities (about 5% each of the grain weight) of two carbohydrates other than starch: pentosans (which make rye flour sticky) and glucans (which also give oats its gelatinous and cholesterol-lowering qualities). Along with their water-insoluble proteins, these carbohydrates contribute to the springy texture of cooked grains. Barley absorbs twice as much water as wheat.

Although barley is not usually thought of as a good grain for making bread, lacking significant gluten proteins, its carbohydrate profile makes it an interesting choice for low-gluten baking. We'll talk about this more in Chapter 19.

US versus European Flours

I've heard many stories recently from people who are sensitive to gluten but were able to eat wheat bread in Europe without suffering the usual reactions. What's the explanation for this? I suspect there's more than one layer to the story. One possibility is the lack of bromate (see Bleached or Unbleached? above) and other bleaching chemicals. There are also several differences in the way flours are processed in Europe, as well as variables in the wheat itself.

Processing

The "extraction rate" of flour is the degree to which a flour has been refined, that is, the percentage of whole grain left in the flour after milling. Whole wheat flour has a 90% extraction rate; most white flour in the US has an extraction rate of 70% to 72%. French bread flour has an extraction rate of 72% to +78%, meaning that it retains a higher percentage of the bran. Home bakers can make an equivalent of French flour by adding a little sifted whole wheat flour to white bread flour.

You may have heard of another French flour called Type 55. Dough made with Type 55 flour, which has less gluten than American bread flour, is able to stretch without springing back; American bread flour's gluten is generally too strong for this kind of extensibility. A good equivalent of Type 55 is a blend of half unbleached bread flour and half unbleached all-purpose flour.

Protein Content and Other Differences in the Wheat

As craft bakers know well, the maximum rising potential of the highest-protein wheat is possible only with mechanical mixing, commercial yeast, and hearth baking. However, strong gluten, high protein, and high water absorption don't work well for European-style open-crumb, crusty breads. The Type 55 French bread flour is typically 11.5% protein, compared with American spring wheat at nearly 14% protein.

The glutenin to gliadin ratio is often different as well. For example, some French flours have a ratio that results in good "thin-film extensibility," allowing stretching without rupture.

European flours have higher ash (mineral) content. Ash significantly stimulates the growth of natural leaven cultures and can be recreated by adding some whole wheat flour to white-flour leavens.

American flours have more damaged starch than European flours due to different milling techniques. This provides food for fermentation but makes it difficult to achieve a really thin crisp crust.

> **SEXY SCIENCE TALK**
>
> ## A Few More Tips
>
> * Self-rising flour contains baking powder at a rate of 5 to 7 grams per 100 grams flour (1 to 1½ teaspoons per cup). It is good for things like biscuits, but don't use it for making bread.
> * I don't recommend adding vital wheat gluten or high-gluten flour to your bread dough, *except* with rye bread.
> * In general, it is best to use the softest wheat that will give you the results you want.

Other Ingredients for Making Bread
Salt

Salt tightens the gluten network and improves bread volume as well as providing flavor. In sourdough breads, salt also helps limit the protein-digesting activity of the lactic bacteria, which can otherwise damage the gluten.

I prefer using sea salt. Be sure to weigh salt, as different types, such as kosher salt, vary in weight relative to volume. When you find a salt you like, stick with that one; it's easiest, especially when you're first learning, to keep things simple.

Yeast

Yeast is a single-cell living organism, the smallest member of the fungus family. Fast-acting yeast allows no time for microbes to do their job, a significant part of which is to disarm gluten molecules while preserving their elasticity.

There are many strains of yeast, one being commercial yeast. By contrast, there are thousands of strains of wild yeast, and the local yeast population varies from region to region. San Francisco is justly famous for its wild yeast, which is responsible for the area's unique sourdough bread. To utilize these wild yeasts, a sourdough culture, or starter, must be cultivated (see Chapters 14 and 15).

The alternative to wild yeast is commercial yeast, usually found in dried form. It can be bought in individual packets or in bulk. It's best to store unused yeast in the freezer; it goes dormant in the cold and will last a good long time.

Active dry yeast, introduced in the 1920s, is dried into granules with a protective coating of yeast debris. These yeast cells are dormant, and must be reactivated by soaking in warm water (105°F to 110°F/41°C to 43°C) before mixing the dough. At cooler soaking temperatures, yeast cells recover poorly and release glutathione, known to interfere with gluten production.

Instant yeast, available since the 1970s, is dried more quickly than active dry yeast, in the form of small porous rods that take up water more rapidly than granules. Instant yeast does not require prehydration before use. It also produces CO_2 more vigorously than other types of yeast. This is definitely my choice among the dry yeasts.

Water

Distinctly acidic water weakens the gluten network in bread dough, while a slightly alkaline water strengthens it. Hard water produces a firmer dough due to the cross-linking effects of calcium and magnesium.

Most tap water from municipal water supplies are slightly alkaline; the chlorine in tap water, though, tends to inhibit yeast growth, so avoid it if you can. If you must use chlorinated water, dechlorinate it first: Run some tap water into a pan or large bowl, and let it sit, uncovered, for at least a few hours or overnight. Most of the chlorine will dissipate. Bringing the water to a boil before letting it sit helps speed up this dissipation.

Bottled spring water is fine. I don't recommend using distilled water; it lacks minerals that benefit the yeast and bacteria during fermentation.

Other Ingredients Often Found in Bread Recipes

Fats, sugar, eggs, and milk products are all common ingredients in bread recipes. None of these are essential in the basic process of making bread, although a few recipes in this book use them. Here is a brief summary of the effect these ingredients have on bread dough:

* Fats and sugar weaken the gluten network.
* Egg proteins coagulate during cooking, but the fat in eggs weakens gluten. Emulsifiers in eggs stabilize bubbles and starch.
* Milk's protein, fat, and acidity all weaken gluten. Milk weakens gluten in bread dough, apparently because of a whey protein, which can be inactivated by scalding (then cooling) the milk before use.

There is obviously much to think about when choosing ingredients for making bread. I have tried many types of wheat and rye flours, played around a bit with barley (although I more often use barley for making beer and whiskey), and am still experimenting a lot with gluten-free grains. I highly recommend starting out with a good unbleached white bread flour and stone-ground whole wheat flour, and getting used to using that before you fill your kitchen with dozens of grains.

When you find a flour that you like to work with and gives you good results, stick with that at least for a while, just to get really comfortable with it. There's a whole world of grains out there, especially if you live in a grain-growing area, but you'll have to trust me that it's better to start small with your ingredient collection. I want this to be fun, even while you're learning, and it won't be so much fun if it seems overwhelming. There's plenty of time. Be easy on yourself and enjoy the process.

Understanding Gluten

I LOVE GLUTEN. That's probably not surprising, considering how much I obviously love making bread. Since you are reading a book about bread, I'm assuming you're prepared to at least be open-minded on the subject of gluten, which has, unfortunately, gotten a lot of negative press in recent years.

There is a lot of science to understanding the role of gluten in bread. In the course of researching this book, I have read dozens of studies and research papers, and while it is all quite interesting to me, I have left much of this information out of this chapter. After hearing your questions at presentations and demonstrations recently, I have a good idea of just what you really want to know about gluten.

One of the best books I've read on the subject—and I have read it at least half a dozen times—is Stephen Yafa's *Grain of Truth: The Real Case For and Against Wheat and Gluten*. I highly recommend this book if you've read books like *Grain Brain* or *Wheat Belly* and are wondering if you'll ever be able to eat wheat bread again. Ultimately, you'll have to choose what works for you, of course; when it comes to your health and well-being, take your time and make informed choices.

What Exactly Is Gluten and How Does It Work?

Gluten is a protein, not a carbohydrate, that is made up of two precursor proteins, *gliadin* and *glutenin*. In dry grain or flour, these are basically inert. Once water is added to the flour, though, the gliadin and glutenin go into action, linking up in a stretchy network of protein chains that enable the dough to expand during fermentation and hold gas bubbles without bursting.

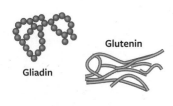

Glutenin

Gliadin

Gluten (Gliadin + Glutenin)

FIGURE 4.1. Diagram of gluten formation.

Wheat dough can expand to hold the CO_2 produced by the yeast because the gluten is both *plastic* and *elastic*. Plasticity is the ability of a substance to change shape under pressure. Elasticity enables a substance to resist pressure and move back toward the original shape once pressure is removed. Thus the dough can expand to accommodate the CO_2 bubbles without its bubble walls stretching to the breaking point.

Plasticity comes from gliadin proteins among the glutenins; elasticity results from the kinky coiled gluten structure. Kneading unfolds and aligns the protein molecules, although some loops and kinks remain. The elasticity relaxes with time (more about this in Chapter 6).

A strong elastic gluten is desirable in yeasted breads; commercial yeast, especially, produces a lot of gas during fermentation, and gluten's elasticity allows the gas bubbles to expand. Too much gluten, though, toughens pastries, raised cakes, and cookies. Intentionally limiting the gluten content, for example by using all-purpose or pastry flour, results in more tender baked goods (see Chapter 19).

Gluten strength is influenced by the kind of flour used, oxidizing agents, and water content of dough (which determines how concentrated the gluten proteins are and how much they are able to bond to each other). Which type of wheat is best suited for a particular kind of cooking or baking depends on the quality of its gluten, not just the protein content.

Protein and gluten qualities of common wheat varieties are listed in the table below. Note that strong protein doesn't always mean strong gluten.

Wheat variety	Percent protein	Gluten quality
Bread	10 to 15	Strong and elastic
Durum	15	Strong, not very elastic
Einkorn	16	Weak and sticky
Emmer (farro)	17	Moderately strong, not very elastic
Hard spelt	16	Moderately strong, not very elastic
Soft spelt	15	Strong, moderately elastic

Source: Harold McGee, *On Food and Cooking*, p. 467

Gluten Grains

It may seem backward, but this chapter includes descriptions of non-gluten grains. See Chapter 3 for more detail on gluten grains; these are the most commonly used grains for bread-making, so I've covered them separately to keep things simple.

Three, and only three, grains contain gluten: **wheat**, **rye**, and **barley**. Wheat has by far the most gluten, which is what makes it the baker's choice for most kinds of bread. Also important is the ratio of gliadin to glutenin; in bread wheat, the ratio of gliadin (which is responsible for plasticity/viscosity) to glutenin (responsible for elasticity) is 1 to 1. Einkorn, by contrast, has a ratio of 2 to 1; the result is a sticky, fluid gluten that's unsuited for bread-making.

But Isn't Gluten Bad for You?

If you have celiac disease, then yes, gluten is really bad for you. Celiac disease, a severe autoimmune reaction to gluten that damages the lining of the small intestine, affects less than 1% of the US population (1 in 133). Non-celiac gluten sensitivities (NCGS) are routinely blamed for abdominal and joint pain, fatigue, headaches, a feeling of "fogginess," bloating, and diarrhea.

If you're wondering whether you have celiac disease, very good testing can determine that. As of this writing, I am not aware of any definitive testing available for any other type of gluten sensitivity or allergy.

I slogged through my mother's copy of Dr. David Perlmutter's *Grain Brain*, one of the main books at the forefront of the anti-gluten movement of recent years. It was difficult to read. I had to keep reminding myself that I was researching. The language is fairly loaded; for example, gluten is referred to as a "modern poison." By the time I read it, I had pored over dozens of studies and research papers, and even to my untrained eye, it was clear that the author included only data that he felt supported his claims.

Just one example: Dr. Perlmutter claims that gluten is to blame for the increasing rate of obesity in the United States. Italians eat more than twice the amount of wheat per capita as Americans do; much of that wheat is in the form of white-flour bread and pasta. So how is it that their obesity rate is only 8.3% while that of Americans is 36%?

Keeping in mind that I am not a medical professional, here's my reaction to *Grain Brain*, boiled down to one sentence: I can't support any premise that relies on nearly 40-year-old research that was never done on humans and blames an astounding laundry list of human ailments on exactly one thing.

Non-gluten Grains

A wide variety of grains have no gluten and thus are safe for celiac disease patients or anyone who has a gluten sensitivity. Here is a summary of the more common gluten-free grains used in baking and cooking. (A more detailed list of gluten-free grains is provided in Chapter 18.)

Oats are rich in indigestible carbohydrates (soluble fiber) called beta-glucans, which absorb and hold water. These are especially concentrated in oat bran and are responsible for the well-documented reputation of oats as a cholesterol-lowering food; regular consumption over a period of weeks has been shown to reduce LDL (low-density lipoproteins, or "bad" cholesterol) levels. Oats are also an excellent source of protein, dietary fiber, B vitamins, and minerals. In addition, oats add flavor and fat to bread doughs, and they improve the shelf life of bread because they prevent fats in the bread from becoming rancid.

Oats contain no gluten, but they do contain avenins, proteins similar to the gliadin protein in wheat. A small percentage of celiac disease

---

SEXY SCIENCE TALK

Allergies Versus Sensitivities

The University of Maryland Center for Celiac Research estimates the number of people worldwide with gluten sensitivity at 6%; a study conducted by Monash University of Melbourne, Australia, estimates the number to be only 0.5%. These numbers stand in stark contrast to the 40% claimed by David Perlmutter, MD, the author of *Grain Brain*.

Not surprisingly, there is a lot of confusing information about gluten sensitivities and allergies. What's the difference? I don't really know. I'm very fortunate to not have any allergy issues currently, but I believe there is a particular histamine reaction to allergens that differentiates allergies from sensitivities. Absent this histamine reaction, the picture gets murkier, with a wide range of symptoms reported by people who believe they suffer from varying degrees of gluten sensitivity.

patients react to avenins, but oats are usually well tolerated by people with non-celiac gluten sensitivities. However, oats are prone to cross-contamination, being often processed in facilities that process gluten grains like wheat and barley; look for oatmeal or oat flour that is labeled "Certified Gluten-free" to avoid problems if you are sensitive to gluten.

Cornmeal and **corn flour** are not the same thing. Cornmeal, or polenta, is coarsely ground from the whole corn kernel; corn flour is the finely ground endosperm of the corn kernel. When finely ground cornmeal is made from whole corn that has been soaked in an alkaline solution (a process known as nixtamalization), it is called masa, and is typically used for making tortillas and tamales. Avoid degerminated cornmeal and corn flours, and refrigerate stone-ground cornmeal and flour.

Millet is an important food staple in Asian and African countries. Pearl millet, the most common, is an excellent source of dietary fiber, protein, several B-complex vitamins, and minerals, especially manganese.

Buckwheat is not related to wheat and is not a grass. It is a member of the rhubarb family and an excellent source of protein, dietary fiber, B vitamins, and minerals; it is especially high in niacin, magnesium, manganese, and phosphorus. It contains about twice the oil of most cereal grains, which limits its shelf life.

Buckwheat contains compounds called fluorescent phototoxic fagopyrins, which can cause severe allergic reactions in some people when buckwheat products make up a significant part of the diet. However, seeds, flour, and teas made from buckwheat are generally safe when consumed in normal amounts.

Quinoa is a flowering plant in the amaranth family. Unlike most grains, it is not a grass, so it is not considered a true cereal. Quinoa is a complete protein source,

---

SEXY SCIENCE TALK

What About Gluten in Liquor?

I included information about gluten in alcoholic beverages in my second book, *Craft Distilling*. I mention this because many people who are avoiding gluten are understandably confused by the labeling of liquor. In fact, there is no gluten in distilled liquor. However, the majority of distilled liquor is made with barley, which does contain gluten. US regulations state that if a product is made from a grain known to contain gluten, it cannot be labeled "gluten-free," even if it can be proved to contain no gluten.

containing all nine essential amino acids. It also contains moderate amounts of dietary fiber and minerals. Cooked quinoa is an excellent source of manganese and phosphorus.

Teff grains are the seeds of an annual grass native to Ethiopia and Eritrea. High in dietary fiber and iron, it is a rich source of manganese and other minerals and also provides protein and calcium. Teff grain and flour can be found in ivory and brown varieties.

Nutrition Concerns with Gluten-free Ingredients

In case you have a bag or two of a commercial gluten-free baking mix in your pantry, consider this. A typical mix might include tapioca, corn and rice flours, potato starch, and xanthan gum (a polysaccharide thickener). These ingredients have one thing in common: They all lack insoluble fiber. They metabolize so quickly that their glucose molecules shoot straight through our gut walls, promoting insulin resistance, obesity, and Type 2 diabetes while adding little, if any, nutritive value.

If you prefer to avoid gluten grains, I suggest using whole-grain gluten-free flours and mixes whenever possible. We've been cautioned for years to minimize our consumption of highly processed white flour. I've been working with several different gluten-free grains and flours, and most of them are just as highly processed as commercial white flour. Rice-based flours and mixes are particularly bad in this regard, with little if any nutritive value left after processing.

When wheat has been germinated for 2 to 3 days, enzymes and chemicals break down large protein chains, also making vitamins A, B, and C more accessible as it releases iron, potassium, and calcium.

According to a 2009 study cited in *Annals of Medicine* (2009, Vol. 41, no. 5), "Germinating wheat enzymes reduce the toxicity of wheat gliadin."

SEXY SCIENCE TALK

What About Sprouted Grains?

The germination process activates enzymes that are proven to break down gluten proteins and carbohydrates. Sprouting also releases phytase and amylase. Phytase makes phosphorus and other minerals bio-available; amylase makes plant material more digestible by humans. "Research studies indicate that enzymatic germination effectively detoxifies gluten molecules [gliadin]."
(*Grain of Truth*, p. 218)

Does Sourdough "Eat" Gluten?

I frequently get asked about this. Quite a few sources say something like this: that sourdough somehow neutralizes or deactivates the gluten in wheat. I'll cover this in more detail in Chapter 14, but here's a quick hit on what I know. First, a little science, then I'll try to explain in a way that makes sense.

Disulfide bonds form bridges between the gliadin storage proteins (prolamins) and, in so doing, give them a compact structure that is difficult to break down by digestive enzymes. Sourdough's lactobacilli act as razors that sever those links and allow digestive enzymes to break down gluten proteins into small amino acid fragments, or peptides.

Wheat contains an enzyme that can cause an allergic reaction. The bit of disulfide reduction and protein degradation from sourdough can be enough to deactivate that enzyme. However, many people who feel they are sensitive to gluten find that they can eat whole-grain, sourdough bread with no negative effects. This can be explained by the findings of scientific studies showing that the lactic bacteria produced during long sourdough fermentation effectively break down gluten molecules. It may also be, of course, that the physical reaction is due to something other than gluten, such as FODMAPs or fructose (see Sexy Science Talk, p. 30).

So What's a Bread Lover to Do?

If you choose to avoid gluten, for whatever reason, does that mean giving up on ever eating bread? These days there are more choices in gluten-free breads available commercially. If you find one you like, that's great. But do consider the tradeoffs of overly processed ingredients and relative lack of nutrition before you swear off wheat-based breads.

Another alternative is to try reducing your gluten intake, either by eating smaller portions or by substituting non-gluten grains for some of the wheat in recipes. This idea doesn't seem to get any attention in the press; everything is either gluten-free or not. In Chapter 19, I will go into much more detail about low-gluten baking and different ways to approach this interesting method.

SEXY SCIENCE TALK

FODMAPs and Fructose Malabsorption

Just a little food for thought, for those of you who are wondering about gluten sensitivity.

FODMAPs, a perfectly justifiable acronym for fermentable oligosaccharides, disaccharides, monosaccharides, and polyols, are carbohydrates found in dozens of fruits and vegetables, as well as in wheat and other grains. These sugars are generally poorly digested, and more and more medical researchers believe that they may actually be responsible for most, if not all, of the intestinal problems frequently attributed to gluten sensitivity. Of FODMAP foods, the fructan carbohydrate is mainly responsible for the intestinal symptoms.

Prebiotics are non-digestible fiber products, important because they promote growth of beneficial intestinal organisms. The FODMAP fractions in wheat are prebiotic, so they are believed to have a positive effect on gut bacteria.

Fructose malabsorption is another possible cause of gut symptoms that are often attributed to gluten intolerance. Fructose is a sugar found in many foods; sucrose (table sugar) is a combination of glucose and fructose. For many people, only a certain amount of fructose, which is digested in the small intestine, can be processed at one time. If more than this amount of fructose is consumed, the small intestine absorbs as much as it can, and the rest goes on to the large intestine, which is not equipped to properly digest it. The most common result is gas, bloating, and diarrhea—which happen to be the most common intestinal symptoms blamed on gluten.

It's important to note that it would be very difficult to completely eliminate foods containing FODMAPs or fructose from the diet; the foods left over, for most people, would not provide adequate nutrition. Here again, moderation may be the key. It can be time-consuming to do an elimination diet in order to discover which food or foods cause these symptoms, but it may make more sense than simply avoiding a long list of otherwise nutritious foods.

Here's the thing: If you feel better when you aren't consuming bread or other products containing gluten, then by all means, avoid those products. But please be honest with yourself: If you've been (or are considering) going gluten-free simply because you've read or heard that gluten is "bad" for you, it's worth considering all the facts and making an informed choice. What I've presented in this chapter is just scratching the surface of all the research that is ongoing around the world.

Now that you understand what gluten is, and its function in the process of bread-baking, let's head into the kitchen and get started!

From Mixing Bowl to Bread Machine: Use What Works for You

Oh, boy. There is so much baking equipment out there. Businesses that cater to home bakers, like King Arthur Flour, offer lots of baking pans, ingredient storage items, and all sorts of gadgets that can make your baking experience even more enjoyable. This chapter includes a summary of items that will get you started, at least, without a huge outlay of cash or that mad scramble to find more storage space in your kitchen or pantry. I'll start with ingredient storage, which doesn't get a lot of time in the spotlight, and go on to your basic toolkit and optional equipment.

Ingredient Storage

I do a lot of baking and have several different flours in my kitchen and pantry, as well as salt, malt powder, honey, seeds and nuts, and whole grains. How do I store all this stuff?

First, there's my beloved Hoosier cabinet. Living in Washington State, I was very fortunate to score this from an eBay seller about an hour away, shortly after moving to the farm. Authentic Hoosier cabinets from Indiana are a lot easier to find east of the Rockies than on the West Coast. It was missing its original flour bin, which I later replaced, and it was worth the extra expense. It holds a full 25 pounds of flour and has a built-in sifter. Flour goes in at the top and out through the sifter at the bottom, so the oldest always gets used first. I use it to hold my unbleached white bread flour, which comes in 50-pound bags;

FIGURE 5.1. My Hoosier cabinet's 25-pound bread bin.

whole wheat flour comes 25 pounds at a time, and I store that, as well as extra bulk grains, in 6-gallon, lidded food-grade buckets.

Smaller quantities of flour, such as some of the gluten-free grains, are stored in half-gallon wide-mouth Mason jars. Quart-sized Mason jars, also wide-mouth, are great for ingredients like salt, seeds, and malt powder. I get my SAF instant yeast in 1-pound bags from King Arthur Flour, but I don't use it very frequently, so it is stored in a pint-sized Mason jar in the freezer.

I know it's recommended to keep some kinds of flour, like rye or whole wheat, refrigerated, but I simply don't have the room in our small propane refrigerator. Our kitchen stays relatively cool, the pantry even more so, and I just do the best I can to keep moisture and heat away from the flour and buy quantities that can be used up promptly.

If you want to grind whole grain yourself, buying in bulk will save money. Be sure to keep it dry and out of the reach of hungry mice and other rodents; a clean bucket with a tight-fitting lid works great if you have more than a few pounds of grain. Be sure the bucket is food-grade, though. Natural food stores that sell a great deal of bulk products get products like honey and molasses in food-grade buckets, and will often give you empty ones if you ask.

Equipment for Bread-making: Your Basic Toolkit

If you do any cooking or baking at all, you probably have most of the basic equipment already. Here's what I have in my primary bread toolkit:

* Kitchen scale (one that measures in 1-gram increments is ideal)
* Mixing bowl and wooden spoon
* 2-quart dough-rising bucket, or other straight-sided clear container with lid
* Large cutting board
* Bannetons or other proofing baskets

FIGURE 5.2. The basic toolkit for home bread-baking.

* Baking stone
* Pizza peel and parchment paper
* Sharp serrated bread knife
* Cooling rack

Kitchen Scales

I highly recommend weighing ingredients rather than measuring them, using metric weights because I find the math is much simpler. I use a small, lightweight battery-powered kitchen scale from Escali, which costs around $30 at King Arthur Flour (see Appendix B). It is very simple to use, can weigh in ounces and pounds as well as grams, and measures down to 1 gram. Well worth the investment!

Mixing Bowls and Wooden Spoons

If you mix your dough by hand, it's simple: All you need is a bowl large enough to hold the ingredients and a wooden spoon for stirring.

Dough-rising Buckets

The 2-quart dough-rising bucket is one of my favorite things for home baking. I love them so much that I buy some before presentations, to give away to the audience. I get mine from King Arthur Flour. What I love about this bucket is that it's the perfect size for my usual 1-loaf batch of bread dough (500 g total flour); with this batch, after I knead the dough I put it in the bucket, put on the lid, and let it ferment. When the dough fills the bucket, it's doubled in volume. So easy! (These buckets come in several sizes; I have a couple of 6-quart buckets I use for larger batches of bread and also to store flour.)

Cutting Boards

You'll need a large cutting board to shape your dough on and to divide it if you're making more than one loaf at a time. I prefer bamboo cutting boards myself, but plastic boards are fine too.

Bannetons and Other Proofing Baskets

I adore my *bannetons*. I know, another French word. They are unfinished, raw willow baskets that hold the fermented dough for proofing after the dough is shaped. I work with a lot of very wet dough, and these baskets help maintain the shape of the loaf as it rises slightly during the proofing process. The best selection (and prices) I've found for these baskets is Lucky Clover Trading Company (see Appendix B); I use several sizes of round and oval bannetons.

Baking Stones

Baking stones come in a variety of sizes, materials, and thicknesses. My fire-clay baking stone is about 15" by 18" and ½" thick; it fits easily on the rack in my gas oven but is large enough to bake two loaves of bread at once. Baking stones enable you to simulate hearth baking in your kitchen oven and are especially useful if you like making crusty, free-form loaves. I recommend thicker stones; they certainly cost more, but mine has lasted for years and I love the results I get from it. Rectangular stones also allow more versatility in terms of the size and shape of loaves they can accommodate.

Pizza Peels and Parchment Paper

Most baking supply stores these days sell at least one type of pizza peel—thin, flat paddles with a handle. Some look like oversized ping-pong paddles, with a metal blade and short handle; others, like mine, are wooden, with long handles. The peel is for transferring loaves of bread into the oven for baking and removing them when they're done. I like to put a piece of parchment paper on my peel, tip the proofed dough from the banneton onto the parchment, and slide it into the oven. The bread bakes on the parchment, and even at high temperatures, I can reuse the parchment at least twice before it's had enough.

Bread Knives or Lames

Especially if you're making free-form loaves, you'll want something to slash the dough with right before putting it in the oven. I bought an inexpensive *lame*, which is basically a double-sided razor blade with a handle, designed for slashing. I suppose this gets easier with practice, but so far I'm not very good at it. What works best for me is a sharp, serrated bread knife. A steak knife would probably work just as well; I do find serrated blades work better, especially with wet doughs.

FIGURE 5.3. Bread knife and lame, tools for scoring loaves before baking.

Incidentally, I also use my bread knife for dividing dough, if I'm making more than one loaf, or rolls or bagels.

Cooling Racks

I prefer stainless steel cooling racks. I bought several, in different sizes, from a local restaurant supply store; they're fairly heavy-duty (strong enough to hold Mason jars of canned food while cooling) and have lasted very well. Wooden racks are fine too, although I find stainless steel easier to keep clean.

Beyond the Basics

Like anything else that happens in the kitchen, once you're comfortable with the basics, you can add to your toolkit as you go along. Here is a short list of gear you might find useful, depending on what kind of bread you make and your preferences for mixing, kneading, and baking:

* Heavy-duty stand mixer, like KitchenAid, with a dough hook for kneading
* Food processor
* Bread machine
* Baking pans (I recommend Pyrex or stainless steel, not non-stick pans)
* Cast-iron Dutch oven with lid
* Clay cloche or other earthenware baking pan

Stand Mixers and Food Processors

Although I have never used a mixer with a hook for kneading dough (I don't own one), I can definitely understand the appeal. I have tendinitis in my elbows, which is likely to appear when I am kneading bread dough by hand. I have come up with a strategy for dealing with this (see Chapter 6) but may add a stand mixer to my toolkit in the future. Aside from physical considerations, mixers do a good job of kneading very wet doughs like *ciabatta* (Chapter 12) and Roman-style pizza (Chapter 13).

Our Cuisinart food processor came with a plastic blade for mixing bread dough. Like mixers, food processors can be especially helpful for mixing very wet doughs.

If you want to knead dough with a stand mixer or food processor, be sure to read the instructions for your particular machine. It's most important to remember that it's easy to over-knead your dough by machine, because the faster pace of the kneading heats the dough more quickly than hand-kneading. More about this in Chapter 6.

Bread Machines

Although our solar electricity has been up and running at the farm since early 2015, I've found that I am still so used to living without electricity that it often doesn't occur to me to use small electric appliances. I've never had a bread machine, but I know several people who love using their machines. As with stand mixers, I can see their appeal, especially if you have a hectic schedule and would otherwise have a hard time fitting bread-making into your day.

Keep in mind that bread machines are designed for white-flour loaves, even if yours has a whole-wheat cycle. *Laurel's Kitchen Bread Book* (see Appendix B) has quite a good primer on making whole-wheat bread using a bread machine, as well as tips for choosing, using, and maintaining your machine.

Bread Pans

Since my husband David generally prefers bread in a traditional loaf shape, being easy to cut into uniform slices for sandwiches and toast, I do sometimes use a standard loaf pan. My favorite is Pyrex, but stainless steel is fine too. I've also seen heavy-duty aluminum bread pans (King Arthur Flour sells this type) but haven't used them myself. I usually avoid aluminum in the kitchen; it reacts with acidic foods, and I'm not sure how it might affect the relatively acidic sourdough. I definitely do not recommend using non-stick pans for baking bread.

Cast-iron Dutch Oven and Other Cast-iron Pans

Baking bread with cast-iron cookware can give some excellent results. I don't have very much experience with it myself, tending to prefer free-form loaves baked either on the hearth in my wood-fired oven (see Chapter 22) or on the baking stone in my kitchen oven. Like a baking stone, the cast iron soaks up the heat of the oven; when it comes in contact with bread dough, the heat causes the gas bubbles in the dough to expand quickly, resulting in good "oven spring." The additional heat also caramelizes the starches in contact with the pan, giving the bread an incredibly delicious crust.

With a Dutch oven, you can bake with the lid on or off. Shortly before finishing this book, when I was speaking at the Mother Earth News Fair in Topeka, KS, an audience member told me he bakes bread in a cast-iron skillet; he simply puts the dough in the lightly oiled skillet after kneading, and lets the dough ferment in the pan before baking.

FIGURE 5.4. Cast-iron Dutch oven and other cast-iron pans useful for baking.

What a great idea! This is a good example of someone who found his comfort zone; this method eliminates the need to shape the bread, the shape and size being defined by the baking pan. It simplified the process for him, making it more fun and easy, and he loves the bread he makes. Perfect!

Clay Cloches and Other Earthenware Pans

The bell-shaped *cloche* (French for "bell") and other earthenware pans, even more than baking stones, simulate hearth baking by surrounding the bread dough with hot clay similar to fire bricks.

Use What Works for *You*

Again, the purpose of this book is to help you find your comfort zone with bread. There is no right or wrong way to do this; if you really want to make bread even occasionally, there is a way to make that work for you. Your comfort zone may change over time. For example, although I still love mixing, kneading, and shaping bread by hand, I might have to change my methods someday, for physical or other reasons. So I think it's great that today we have choices like bread machines and stand mixers. It might take some time, but you will find your comfort zone, and you will enjoy baking bread. Hurray!

How to Make Dough:
The Gentle Art of Fermentation

THE DEVELOPMENT OF bread dough, involving the mixing, kneading, fermentation, and proofing, is where most of the science of bread baking happens. It's arguably the most important part of the whole process. While I think it is helpful to understand at least some of the science involved, you won't be able to read the book if your eyes are glazed over or you're bored to tears. So let's keep this as simple as possible.

What Is Dough, Anyway?

Dough structure is composed of three basic elements: water, gluten proteins, and starch granules. Bread is light and tender because the protein-starch mass is divided up by the millions of tiny bubbles produced during fermentation. When dough is cooked, starch granules absorb water, swell, and create a solid structure, a sponge-like network of starch and protein filled with tiny air pockets. This network of starch, protein, and air pockets is called the crumb.

In order to rise, dough must be leavened. The purpose of leavening is to produce gas bubbles. Some breads, like quick breads, are leavened chemically, with baking soda or baking powder. Most of the breads in this book are leavened with yeast, either commercial yeast or the wild yeasts relied on in the production of sourdough bread.

Bread dough rises during fermentation and baking because gas is trapped in the dough. Gas production is about the same for wheat and rye, but gas retention quality is much better in wheat because of its gluten content, which is much higher than that of rye.

Measuring Ingredients: The Baker's Percentage

The concept of the baker's percentage makes sense when you weigh ingredients rather than measuring them. For commercial bakers, who work with hundreds of pounds of flour at a time, it's an indispensable tool. Simply, the baker's percentage calculates the weight of each ingredient, as a percentage of the total amount of flour used. So if a baker starts with a 100-pound sack of flour, the baker's percentage accurately tells her how much salt and leaven to add and the correct amount of water to achieve the desired level of hydration.

I know you're wondering if this is actually important for a home baker. If you only ever want to follow existing recipes, including those in this book, it's not really necessary. But if you want to concoct your own recipes, or improvise variations on some other recipe, such as changing the hydration rate, then it's very helpful to understand this concept.

Each recipe in this book includes the baker's percentage of each ingredient, so you can get used to the idea even if you never use it. Just keep in mind that it is always based on the *total* amount of flour in the recipe. In the spirit of maintaining simplicity, most of these recipes follow the same simple formula calling for a total of 500 grams of flour.

Here's a simple example, using 1,000 grams of flour. Say I want a dough of 65% hydration, with a normal amount of salt. A typical amount is 2% by weight, so I would add 20 grams of salt (20 being 2% of 1,000, the amount of flour). You've no doubt guessed that you will add 650 grams of water.

You math whizzes out there will note that this dough is not 65% water; with 1,000 grams flour, 650 grams water, and 20 grams salt, there is a total weight of 1670 grams. So, *by weight*, the dough is actually about 39% water, about 60% flour, and just over 1% salt.

This reminds me of the somewhat dubious math used in major league baseball to calculate how many games behind or ahead each team is. You know, "The Fighting Sand Crabs of Tukwila are now 12 games over 500!" I remember my dad pitching a mild fit about this every year during Mariners games, and he was right. Ooh, more sexy science talk...

Mixing Dough

I prefer mixing my dough with cool water, not warm, especially when making long-fermenting sourdough. Even with yeast breads, I rarely use active dry yeast, opting instead for instant yeast; hydrating the yeast in warm water before mixing the dough isn't necessary. Ideally, the dough stays relatively cool during mixing and kneading, about 76° to 80°F (24° to 26°C), so using water that is no warmer than room temperature is best. Kneaded by hand, the dough increases in temperature by up to one degree per minute, twice that when kneading with a mixer and dough hook.

The Autolyze Process

The French can make anything sound sexy, and they make damned good bread. I admit, at first I was skeptical about how much difference the autolyze process would make. Gosh. Let's just say, it makes a big difference, especially if you knead the dough by hand.

Although it sounds fancy, all that's involved in the *autolyze* process (autolysis means "self-digestion") is mixing the flour with water and letting it rest for 15 to 20 minutes before kneading. According to French bread expert Raymond Calvel, giving the starches and gluten proteins a chance to absorb as much water as possible, without the interference of salt, allows the gluten chains to develop during the rest period. The dough is then easier to knead, and less kneading is required.

High-protein flours, for example, whole wheat flour, require more hydration in dough and especially benefit from the autolyze process.

Kneading

Kneading is a process of repeatedly stretching, folding, and compressing dough. This strengthens the gluten network by aligning the proteins

TIP
A good rule of thumb for measuring flour: If you're weighing the flour, weigh it *before* you sift. If you're measuring it, measure *after* sifting.

side to side and promoting formation of weak bonds. End-to-end bonds also form, creating the network of gluten chains. Kneading also aerates the dough, providing oxygen to the yeast during fermentation.

I prefer kneading dough by hand. I like feeling the dough in my hands; you can actually feel the gluten developing and the dough becoming more stretchy and cohesive. Hand-kneading virtually eliminates any worry about overheating the dough and compromising the gluten, simply because the slower tempo keeps the dough cool. You'll develop your own rhythm when kneading, whatever is most comfortable. There's no hurry; you'll get the hang of it with a little practice.

How do you keep dough from becoming too dry during kneading? When you turn the dough out on a board or your counter to knead, it's way too easy to stiffen the dough by flouring your hands when they become sticky; this obviously adds flour to the dough, changes the hydration rate, and usually results in finished bread that is dry and crumbly. My favorite technique when kneading is to have a small bowl of cool water next to the mixing bowl with the bread dough. Whenever the dough starts to stick to my hands, I dip my kneading hand in the cool water and proceed. This helps ensure proper hydration of all the grains in the dough, as well as a finished bread that is moist and has excellent keeping qualities.

TIP

I usually wear latex-free nitrile gloves while kneading. I find the dough sticks a lot less to my hands when they are gloved. I have mixed feelings about using disposable gloves, but as my skin is somewhat sensitive, I enjoy the bread-making process more when my hands are protected. Again, choose what works for you.

Kneading by machine must be done carefully, in order to avoid overheating the dough, which would break down the gluten. This is especially true of kneading with a food processor (see Chapter 5 for more on machine kneading).

How Your Muscles Are Like Gluten

Is it true that the longer you knead dough, the more gluten develops? Well, to a point, yes. It's important to understand that kneading doesn't create gluten;

FIGURE 6.1. Dough after kneading.

SEXY SCIENCE TALK

The Magical Molecular Movement of Gluten Proteins

Gliadin and glutenin, gluten's precursor proteins, don't dissolve in water; when dry, they are immobile and inert. When moistened, however, the protein molecules bind to the surface of starch granules; they change shape, move around relative to each other, and form and break bonds with each other. Dough becomes more elastic as gluten is formed, because gluten molecules are coiled and very kinky. When the dough is stretched during kneading, the kinks straighten out; when released, kinks and coils reform and dough shrinks back.

TIP

If you're kneading dough with a stand mixer, it's a good idea to cut the protein content a bit by substituting all-purpose flour for part of the bread flour.

it merely exercises the gluten that is already present. Just like human muscles, actually: Everyone is born with a given number of muscle cells, which partly explains why some of us are world-class sprinters and weight-lifters, and most of us aren't. Exercising our muscles doesn't increase the number of muscle cells we have; it simply increases the size of those cells. As any athlete knows, if you have an injury that prevents you from exercising for some length of time, those muscle cells shrink. So now when you knead your bread dough by hand, remember that you're exercising your muscles as well as all that gluten.

Fermentation

Just to clarify, in this book I use the term fermentation to describe the rising process of bread dough; that is, what happens between kneading the dough and baking it. There are usually two stages to fermentation: The primary rise (between kneading and shaping the dough); and the secondary rise, or proofing stage (between shaping the loaf and baking).

Most of the flavor development happens during the primary fermentation, especially with long-fermented bread like sourdough. During this stage, the activity of the yeast and lactobacillus bacteria in the dough is quite enthusiastic; the yeast is multiplying rapidly, producing the gas bubbles apparent in the rising of the dough. Meanwhile, the bacteria are gradually producing lactic acids that contribute to the flavor and aroma of the bread.

What's going on during fermentation? In any fermented food, yeast consumes sugar, producing alcohol and carbon dioxide (CO_2) in the process. The CO_2 bubbles that form expand during fermentation and are trapped by the stretchy bands of gluten proteins, allowing the dough to rise. The amount of time this process takes varies greatly, depending on type of yeast (wild or commercial), fermentation temperature, and other factors. For example, a typical bread made with commercial yeast might take only about 4 hours from start to finish; my usual routine with sourdough bread, which relies on wild yeast, takes 24 hours or more.

FIGURE 6.2. Dough in dough-rising bucket at start of fermentation.

FIGURE 6.3. Fermented dough ready to shape and proof.

Retarding the Dough

Retarding fermentation (usually in a refrigerator) slows the activity of microbes; yeasts can take up to 10 times as long to raise dough. This increase in fermentation time allows yeasts and bacteria to produce more flavor compounds. Cold dough is also easier to shape because it is stiffer, so it's easier to handle without losing too much of its leavening gas. Retarding also allows for more flexibility in your baking schedule; if something comes up, and your baking plan is interrupted, you can always put the dough in the fridge and finish it hours or even a day or two later.

Peter Reinhart's lovely book *Crust and Crumb* (see Appendix B) includes lots of wonderful recipes for fairly experienced bread bakers, many of which call for retarding the dough. I don't use this technique very much, simply because our off-grid propane refrigerator is about half the size of an average fridge, and most of the time there isn't room for a large tub of bread dough. I do like to refrigerate fairly wet doughs like my bagel dough (see Chapter 9), as the dough is easier to handle and shape when it's cold. Keep in mind that the yeast and bacteria are still at work, just at a slower pace than at room temperature.

A Slightly More Advanced Technique: Gelatinizing Starch by Scalding the Flour

Some of the ungelatinized starch in flour is not utilized well by amylase, the enzyme that breaks down starch into fermentable sugars that yeast feeds on during the fermentation process.

Scalding a small proportion of the flour, say 10%, with boiling water bursts the starch granules, making more food available to yeast cells for the production of

---

SEXY SCIENCE TALK

Geeking Out on Yeast Metabolism

In unsweetened dough, yeasts grow on the single-unit sugars glucose and fructose and on the double-glucose sugar maltose, which enzymes in the flour produce from broken starch granules.

Here's the oh-so-fascinating equation for the conversion that happens in yeast metabolism:

$$C_6H_{12}O_6 \rightarrow 2C_2H_5OH \rightarrow 2CO_2$$

(Or, in something more closely resembling plain English: 1 molecule of glucose yields 2 molecules of alcohol plus 2 molecules of carbon dioxide.)

SEXY SCIENCE TALK

How Do Your Microbes Grow?

There are three stages of microbial growth during fermentation: the lag phase, during which no growth is observed; the logarhythmic phase (fast growth); and the static phase (organisms have run out of food or are inhibited by metabolic end products like acetic acid).

Optimum temperature for growth of sourdough lactobacilli is 89° to 91°F (32° to 33°C), with pH 5.0 to 5.5 (min. 3.8). For yeast, optimum temperature for overall growth is 82°F (28°C), although yeast cells grow and produce gas most rapidly at about 95°F (35°C). Yeast activity also contributes chemicals that strengthen the gluten and improve elasticity.

CO_2. It also increases the hydration of the dough, resulting in a bread with a more tender crumb and better shelf life. Try this with whole-grain pizza dough and with lower-protein flours like all-purpose flour.

To scald, put the flour to be scalded in a mixing bowl. Set the bowl on a trivet or hot pad; the bowl will get hot when you pour boiling water on the flour. Ideally, measure the boiling water, remembering to subtract this amount from the total water called for in the recipe. As you gain experience working with fairly wet doughs, you will find that you can just stir in enough boiling water to make a flour-water mixture about the consistency of pancake batter. This doesn't take a lot of water and won't significantly change the hydration rate in your dough.

Incidentally, I am currently experimenting with scalding as a way to improve gluten-free breads. As I write this, I don't have very much experience with this less-common technique, but it is very interesting to see the difference it makes in the bread-making process.

Can We Get to Actually Making the Bread Now?

Now that you've mixed, kneaded, and fermented your dough, it's time to move on to shaping, proofing, and baking the bread. With breads like sourdough, which are fermented over a period of hours, this last bit might seem like the very tip of an enormous iceberg. I promise you, this feeling will fade as you get comfortable with your bread-making routine and gain some confidence in yourself as a bread baker. Remember, the actual hands-on work is a small part of the process; the rest of the time, the magical process of fermentation is constantly in motion, turning dry, inert grain into a fragrant, bubbly dough on its way to becoming a beautiful, nutritious loaf of bread, hand-made by *you*.

Shaping, Proofing, and Baking Bread

The smell of good bread baking,
like the sound of lightly flowing water,
is indescribable in its evocation of innocence and delight.
— M.F.K. FISHER

THIS IS ARGUABLY the fun part of making bread: shaping, proofing, and baking. After all the time spent mixing, kneading, and fermenting, especially all the hours involved in long-fermented sourdough bread, this last bit goes fairly quickly. While the processes are fairly straightforward, your ultimate results can vary a lot if you choose to tweak a detail here and there. Bread bakes differently in a pan compared to free-form loaves on a baking stone. Proofing temperature, explained below, as well as baking temperature, can make a big difference. You can use steam, or not, while baking. As with all parts of the bread-baking process, I suggest you stick with the basics until you feel comfortable and confident before you start improvising.

Shaping Dough

Wheat dough can be shaped only because the elasticity relaxes over time. Protein molecules form weak bonds, so eventually the tension in the ball of dough breaks down some of those bonds. I've found it is easier to shape dough that has been fermented overnight or for at least

FIGURE 7.1. Assortment of proofing baskets called bannetons.

8 hours, as with most sourdough breads. With yeast breads, the fermentation process goes so much more quickly that the gluten bonds have barely finished developing by the time you want to shape the dough.

Of course, there are many possible shapes of bread loaves, especially if you like to make them free-form. A simple round, or *boule*, shape is probably the easiest to learn; I most often make an oblong loaf that satisfies my liking for free-form shaping as well as David's preference for one that is easy to slice for toast. Dough can be divided into

FIGURE 7.2. Dough proofing in banneton.

pieces and braided; formed into long thin *baguettes*, or football-shaped *batards*; shaped into round or oblong rolls and buns; and a lot more. If you are brand new to baking bread, I suggest you start by using a loaf pan; this will give you some practice at shaping dough without having to worry about getting fancy shapes right. The confines of the pan also help ensure a good rise in the oven (especially important if you are baking low- or no-gluten breads, as explained in Chapter 19).

Other than the desired loaf shape, the main point of the shaping process is to stretch the gluten strands in the dough so that the loaf will hold that shape throughout baking. The tricky thing is to stretch the gluten enough to accomplish this, without over-handling the dough to the point where the gas bubbles burst. Loss of some gas bubbles is unavoidable, and the remaining bubbles will expand again during the proofing process, but the idea is to try to minimize the wholesale loss of too much of that CO_2.

Proofing

Proofing, also called the second rise or second fermentation, is the relatively brief time the dough continues fermenting between shaping and putting it in the oven. Many bakers feel that the trickiest part of making bread is knowing when it is ready to go into the oven. I can tell you, from my own experience, that this isn't something you have to figure out every time you bake bread. In my cool kitchen, the dough proofs darn near perfectly in the hour I am preheating the oven and baking stone. (I make mostly sourdough breads, which ferment and proof relatively slowly; some yeast breads proof more quickly.)

After you've shaped your dough and put it in your banneton (see Chapter 5) or loaf pan, cover it loosely with plastic wrap or a clean kitchen towel and leave it to proof at room temperature. Be sure to start preheating your oven now, especially if you're using a baking stone; the dough may proof faster than you expect, especially during warm weather, and it's better to err on the side of under-proofing than over-proofing. If dough over-proofs, which is a lot more likely with yeast doughs than sourdough doughs, it will collapse when you slash

FIGURE 7.3. Scored loaf ready to bake

it and won't rise well in the oven. I had this happen just the other day, when a yeast bread was proofing while I got engrossed in writing a chapter of this book and frankly just forgot about it. It was still good, but not quite as pretty as it would have been if I had been paying more attention.

How do you know when it's finished proofing and ready to bake? The dough should look very smooth, and it will have expanded, although it might not double in volume during this stage. Wetter doughs like ciabatta and Roman-style pizza will look bubbly and airy and usually inflate more than firmer doughs. Press the pad of your thumb or finger gently onto the surface of the dough; the depression should spring back but slowly. Again, if you're not sure, it's better to put it in the oven a little sooner to avoid over-proofing.

Slashing or Scoring the Loaf

Most free-form loaves benefit from slashing or scoring before baking. Slashing is obviously decorative, but it's also meant to control the way the dough expands in the first few minutes in the oven. You can use a lame, which is basically a curved double-sided razor blade held securely in a handle, or (as I prefer) use a sharp serrated bread knife. There are many different ways to slash, and it's largely up to you. Like other bread-baking skills, slashing will seem easy and effortless after a few rounds of practice. The main thing is to aim to slash between ¼" and ½" deep and use a swift, confident stroke.

For free-form loaves, first tip the loaf out of the banneton onto the parchment paper on your peel (if using a baking stone) or baking sheet. You want to get it into the oven quickly, so be ready to slash as soon as it's on the peel. I make a lot of oblong loaves, not so many round ones, and I like to make several fairly parallel slashes at an angle across the loaf. Round loaves can be slashed in a tic-tac-toe pattern, or with parallel cuts, or across the corners (Figure 7.4).

If you're using loaf pans, I suggest one long slash going lengthwise down the middle of the loaf. I have made plenty of pan loaves where I have forgotten to slash, though, and they turned out just fine in spite of me. So try slashing or skipping it, and see for yourself which results you like the best.

FIGURE 7.4. Baked whole-wheat *miche* showing score marks.

That Poor, Maligned, Misunderstood Starch

The structure of a cooled loaf of bread, regardless of what grain is used, comes from gelatinized starch. This gel forms when starch is heated to a critical temperature in the presence of water. At the point of gelatinization, the starch uncoils from its crystalline structure, breaks out of its granule, and traps water in its "arms."

Gelled starch is essentially dissolved in the trapped water, becoming vulnerable to breakdown by amylase. Before this point, only the starch damaged by milling is susceptible to amylase.

So how does a sturdy structure of gelatinized starch form in wheat bread and then stay intact until the bread has cooled? Most of the amylase is denatured by heat before the starch is gelatinized. Wheat amylase is less heat-stable than rye amylase. However, the high acid content of rye-based sourdough inhibits the amylase activity. That's why all traditional rye breads are made from sourdoughs; the low pH protects the starch gels until the amylase is denatured during baking.

Baking

Later on we'll talk about baking in a wood-fired oven. For now, we'll focus on baking in your kitchen oven. Other than the amount of preheating time needed, baking is pretty much the same for gas and electric ovens.

There are several different ways of baking loaf breads. You can make free-form loaves, shaped by hand and baked on a baking stone or baking sheet. There are standard loaf pans, if you'd rather make loaves of a uniform size and shape that are easy to slice for toast or sandwiches. Other options include baking bread in a cast-iron skillet or Dutch oven, or in a clay or ceramic cloche or other earthenware pot.

If you're using a baking stone, cast-iron pot or an earthenware pot, it's important to adequately preheat the stone or pot before baking. My baking stone is comparatively thick, about ½", and I like to preheat it for a full hour. Preheat cast iron for 30 minutes; clay and ceramic pots will usually preheat in 30 to 45 minutes, depending on how thick the walls are.

What Exactly Happens During Baking?

When breads and cakes are baking, starch granules absorb water, swell, and set to form the rigid bulk of the walls that surround the CO_2 bubbles. This rigidity limits the expansion of the bubbles, forcing water vapor to pop some of the bubbles and escape, creating a continuous spongy network of connected holes. The more CO_2 produced during the preparation of the dough or batter, the more tender the result.

Both the CO_2 and alcohol produced during fermentation are trapped by the dough, but both are expelled from the dough by the heat of baking.

Before I started seriously studying the baking of bread, I wondered why the dough rises only so much in the oven and no higher. It's pretty simple, actually: First, bread yeast starts to die off at about 140°F (60°C). Also, about the same time as the yeast is expiring, the oven heat (especially in a wood-fired oven) will have dried the outer crust of the bread enough so that it is simply not flexible enough to expand any more.

The combination of high heat (450°F/232°C or more) and a thoroughly preheated baking stone combine to create what's called oven spring, the amount the bread rises in the oven. When the dough hits that hot stone, the gas bubbles in the dough expand very rapidly, forcing the dough upward. Virtually all of this oven spring happens in the first 20 minutes or so of baking; after this point, the internal temperature of the dough will be hot enough to kill off the remaining yeast.

What About Using Steam During Baking?

This is something that is often talked about, but I hardly ever do it. In my kitchen oven, it's really hard to tell the difference in the results. The theory of using steam is that the high heat begins to dry out the crust fairly quickly as the dough expands in the early part of baking. Adding steam is meant to keep the surface of the dough moist enough to allow it to rise a little further before the crust dries to the point where it won't expand any more. The dough has only about 20 minutes to rise anyway, as explained above, so if you're going to use steam, it has to be done right when the bread goes into the oven.

When I do remember to use steam, here's what I like to do. When I start preheating the baking stone, I put a small cast-iron skillet on the rack beneath it, where it gets good and hot. I make sure the teakettle is on the woodstove or a gas burner, and the water in it is good and hot. I slide the loaf onto the baking stone and immediately pour some boiling water into the cast-iron skillet and close the oven door quickly. The hot water rapidly produces steam when it hits the hot skillet.

I know a lot of sources suggest using ice cubes, but I don't recommend using ice to create steam. It takes a lot less energy to turn hot water into steam than to turn frozen water into steam, I promise. The main thing is to get the loaves into the oven and the hot water into that cast-iron pan as quickly as possible, and close the door to minimize heat loss.

I'm not sure I have ever tried using steam when baking a yeast bread; I've only ever done that with sourdough. It's possible that there will be more noticeable results with faster-rising yeast breads, I don't know. Oh goody, another thing to experiment with! You know, in all your spare time.

SEXY SCIENCE TALK

Why Isn't Bread Boozy?

Since alcohol is one by-product of fermentation, there ought to be booze in the bread, right? Well, yes, except… both CO_2 and alcohol are expelled from the dough by the heat of baking. Long-fermented dough, and ripe starter, can certainly have a slightly beery aroma. As you know from reading *Craft Distilling*, ethyl alcohol (ethanol) vaporizes at about 173°F (78°C); the internal temperature of bread dough rises to 200°F (93°C) or a little more during the baking process, so the alcohol literally cooks out of the bread. In the case of dough that has beer or other alcohol added to it, the baked bread may retain some of the malty flavor of the beer but not the alcohol. Sorry about that.

How Do You Know When the Bread Is Done?

Most loaf breads are done when the internal temperature is at least 190°F (87°C); closer to 200°F (93°C) is better. I know you've been told to thump the loaf on the bottom and listen for that "hollow" sound; that's a good rule, if anyone can agree on what "hollow" sounds like. My feeling is it's subjective at best. It's great if you have a baking friend who can help you with your first few loaves, until you get the feel of it. You can check the internal temperature with an instant-read thermometer if you want, but I would also gently squeeze the loaf, using a potholder or kitchen towel to hold it. If the crust is set, it will resist squeezing; if it gives, bake it for another 5 minutes and test again.

Cooling and Storing Your Bread

For most breads, it's best to cool the loaves completely on a wire or wooden cooling rack before cutting. I like to cool bread for at least an hour, although there are sometimes exceptions; Montreal bagels (Chapter 9) come to mind. No force on Earth can make me wait an hour to eat one of those! In general, loaf breads keep better if they are cooled before cutting; cutting them while they're hot lets moisture out in the form of steam, so the bread dries out more quickly. Still, it's up to you. If you think you're going to eat up that bread in a day or two anyway, then maybe the additional shelf life doesn't really matter.

Before the bread is cut, you can store it in a paper bag. Once it's cut, though, store it in a food-grade plastic bag. After reusing plastic produce bags a few too many times for my bread, I finally started buying plastic bread bags. They come in different sizes, you don't have to rinse them out and dry them before use, and you can buy 100 at a time if you want. Good sources are King Arthur Flour (kingarthurflour.com) and PaperMart (papermart.com).

Keeping the Process Simple in Spite of the Science Stuff

It would be a lot easier if I could just lay down one hard-and-fast rule and a master baking formula that would work for everyone, every time, but there are way too many possible variables. I have done my best, though, to standardize the recipes in this book. Most of the bread recipes I use are based on 500 grams of flour, so most of the recipes included follow this formula. Unless the dough is enriched with egg, milk, or fats, I generally bake free-form loaf breads at 475°F (246°C). Most bread in pans can be baked at 400° to 425°F (204° to 218°C).

You've just absorbed a lot of information. It might seem overwhelming right now, like there is too much to learn. Remember when you learned to drive a car? It was 40 years ago that I was in driver's ed, fitting in the afternoon classes before basketball practice. I can hardly remember anything I learned in that class; nearly all I know about driving I've learned in the years since that class, by practicing and gaining experience.

So it is with making bread. As you gain experience, you will find your rhythm within your comfort zone. Soon it will all be so familiar that you won't be thrown by last-minute schedule meltdowns or whatever might come up. Dough is pretty resilient; you can always slow down the process by putting it in the fridge, taking a breath, and getting back to it when it's the right time. Remember, it's flour, salt, yeast, and water, not an exotic hothouse plant that might die at any minute for lack of proper attention.

PART TWO

YEAST BREADS

Comfort Zone I:
No-knead Breads

OKAY! You're new to baking bread. You've read "How to use this book." You want to jump right into baking bread without cluttering up your brain with a lot of details about grains and dough development and the perfect way to score a loaf. Probably you've seen articles or read a book about no-knead bread (see Appendix B), and this seems like a good place to start. That's cool. Let's do it!

First, be assured that you can—and will—make wonderful bread without having to understand all the scintillating scientific minutiae about yeast and all that. However, I do think it's helpful to cover a little bit of background information. It's kind of like driving a car: You can do it without being trained as a mechanic, but knowing a few basics like why your car needs a battery and fuel tends to help.

Like any other yeast bread, simple no-knead bread requires four ingredients: **flour**, **water**, **salt**, and **yeast**. No sugar. No milk. No eggs. Just flour (in this case, wheat flour), water, salt, and yeast. We'll get into sourdough later, when you're ready to move to another comfort zone, but for now we're using commercial yeast. (See Chapter 3 for recommendations.)

Quick review: Yeast is a tiny living organism that eats sugar and produces alcohol and carbon dioxide in a process called fermentation. It's what makes bread dough rise, before and during baking. Wheat flour contains proteins that form gluten when water comes in contact with the grain. (See Sexy Science Talk on page 45 for a more detailed description of this process.) Gluten, from the Greek word for glue, is a stretchy protein network that enables wheat dough to keep its structural integrity while rising; without this gluten, the dough is soft, not stretchy, and it doesn't rise much.

What does all this have to do with kneading? Well, the reason for kneading bread dough is to "exercise" the gluten, in order to fully develop its elasticity and strength. To a point, kneading does result in improved texture in the finished bread. So why does this no-knead technique work at all, much less reward you with gorgeous, delicious, beautifully risen loaves? It works because, as we've already discovered, once you add water to that flour, the gluten begins to form its magical network of stretchy cells. So you'll find, with your very first batch, that even without the additional exercise that kneading gives those little gluten molecules, enough gluten forms during the mixing process to allow the bread dough to rise and bake beautifully without collapsing on itself.

Let's get started on a no-knead wheat bread, a simple sandwich bread with 30% whole wheat flour and 70% bread flour. Try this basic recipe first; then if you want to, try one of the variations that follow.

TIP

The less time spent mixing and kneading dough, the longer the fermentation time should be. Wetter dough needs more kneading and longer fermentation times.

SEXY SCIENCE TALK

Energize Dough Fermentation with Rye Flour

Adding a little rye to wheat dough boosts fermentation by liberating more sugar through amylase activity. As long as the pH doesn't drop too low during fermentation, this kind of bread shows better volume and keeping qualities.

No-knead Wheat Bread

Timing

- 3 to 5 minutes to measure ingredients and mix dough
- 20 minutes for autolyze phase
- 1 to 2 hours to ferment dough
- 1 hour to proof dough
- 35 to 45 minutes to bake

Equipment you'll definitely need

- Large mixing bowl (stainless steel, glass, Pyrex, or ceramic)
- Wooden spoon

Stuff that's not absolutely necessary but recommended

- Kitchen scale
- 2-quart dough-rising bucket
- 8" round proofing basket
- Serrated bread knife or single-edge razor blade for slashing dough

Ingredients	Metric	US	Baker's %
• Unchlorinated water, lukewarm	350 g	1½ cups	70
• Unbleached bread flour	350 g	2¼ cups	70
• Whole wheat flour, preferably stone-ground	150 g	1 cup	30
• SAF or other instant yeast	4 g	1 tsp	1
• Sea salt	10 g	1½ tsp	2

Mixing and Fermenting the Dough

Measure the water and yeast into the mixing bowl, stirring to dissolve the yeast. Add the flours and salt, and stir with the wooden spoon for a minute or two. See how that dough is already starting to feel a little bit

FIGURE 8.1. No-knead dough after mixing.

stretchy? Keep stirring. It should be starting to come together in a solid but soft mass. Yay! The gluten is forming!

Now let the dough rest for about 20 minutes; leave the spoon in the dough. You can cover it with plastic wrap if you want to, but it's not necessary. After it's rested (maybe you did too?), stir it again briefly. Can you feel the difference? You can stir it at a leisurely pace now for another couple of minutes if you want to— aha, I tricked you into kneading it a little!— or you can just cover the bowl with plastic wrap and go throw horseshoes out back for a bit while it ferments. (If you have a dough-rising bucket, use the spoon to scrape the dough out of the bowl and into the bucket. Put the lid on and you're done for now.)

TIP

I highly recommend fermenting your dough at a fairly cool temperature; 65° to 68°F (18° to 20°C) is ideal. Slowing down the fermentation just a bit is easier on your schedule; also, the longer it ferments, the more flavor develops. The dough-rising bucket makes it so simple to know when the fermentation is nearing completion: A batch like this, made with 500 grams total of flour, will pretty much fill up that bucket when it doubles in volume.

Shaping and Proofing the Dough

So your dough is fermented. You know it's fermented because it's doubled in size, and has a lovely yeasty, slightly tangy aroma. Now what? Shape, proof, and bake, that's what. In the spirit of this comfort zone, let's keep the shaping part as simple as possible.

Did you notice that I haven't yet told you to punch down your dough? That's because I don't *want* you to punch down your dough! You've just spent at least a couple hours of your day mixing and fermenting the stuff, and it's doubled in volume. Remember all those hungry little yeast cells that have been gobbling up the carbohydrates in the flour; the dough has risen because of all the carbon dioxide bubbles produced during this fermentation process. If you "punch" that dough, guess what happens to all those bubbles? That's right, they BURST. Trust me, you don't want that to happen.

Okay, here's what you want to do. First toss a generous amount of bread flour on a good-sized cutting board (or a clean countertop, if you prefer). Take the lid or plastic wrap off your bread dough and tip the

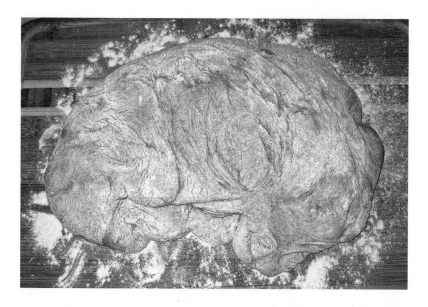

FIGURE 8.2. Fermented dough, just before shaping.

bucket or bowl up so the dough starts sliding out onto the board, using your free hand to help. Some of the bubbles with break as you do this; it's inevitable, but don't worry about it.

At this time, handle the dough gently and not for very long—keeping in mind all the tiny bubbles. The dough will be quite soft. In fact, you may be wondering how on Earth that wet mass of dough will ever form something that looks like a loaf of bread. Bear with me here; you can do this, I promise. Toss a little bread flour over the top of the dough. Now slide one hand under the far edge of the dough, lift up your hand an inch or two and bring that hand toward you, pulling very gently to slightly stretch the dough. You're folding part of the dough mass over the rest of it; does that make sense?

Now repeat those steps a couple more times, picking up and folding over a different part of the dough mass. After just a few rounds, you should find the dough is coming together in a much more smooth-looking ball. I should mention that no matter how many times I make a particular recipe, there is something slightly different about the result every time. I've never figured out why, and I gave up long ago trying to understand it. The point is, don't expect it to look perfect. It hardly

TIP

I like to wear nitrile gloves for the shaping process; I find the dough doesn't stick to the gloves anywhere near as much as it sticks to my hands. The less you manhandle the dough now, the better.

FIGURE 8.3. Dough after shaping.

ever does. You will get better at this; these motions with the hands will feel more natural; you'll get used to how the dough feels as you shape it. Just don't stress right now about that dough ball looking exactly like the one in the photo, okay?

If you have a banneton or proofing basket, dust the inside with flour and gently lift the dough ball and put it into the basket. No proofing basket? It's perfectly fine to line a mixing bowl with a clean dish towel; linen is ideal for this. (Before I bought some proofing baskets, I "borrowed" some of David's nice linen napkins for this, and it worked great.) Be sure to dust the dish towel with flour before putting the dough in there. You can also put it in a greased loaf pan if you prefer. Cover the container with plastic wrap.

So now comes the "proofing" stage. I will cut to the chase here and say that you

T I P

I have often thought that this is the trickiest part of baking bread: judging when the dough is ready to put in the oven. It has helped me to consistently make the same size batch of dough; over time (and a lot of trial and error) I've gotten used to how much the dough rises in the proofing basket before it is baked. It is better to err on the side of under- rather than over-proofing!

FIGURE 8.4. Mixing bowls and baskets lined with muslin or linen work well for proofing dough.

do *not* need a proofing cabinet or any other special apparatus or gizmo for this process. Right now, there is plenty of time, and time = flavor. You need some time to preheat your oven anyway, so just set aside the bread pan or proofing basket; like fermentation, a relatively cool temperature is your friend here. It's okay if it's warmer than 70°F (21°C), just be aware that you will need to watch the dough so it doesn't rise too much before you put it in the oven.

Baking the Bread

For free-form loaves, I highly recommend using a baking stone, a good thick one. In my kitchen, which is quite consistently less than 70°F (21°C), I like to turn on the oven, then shape the dough. I've found that the hour that it takes to thoroughly heat up that baking stone is the perfect amount of time to proof that dough. Be aware that the dough will not double this time; it may get to about 1½ times its original volume, but it won't double. You don't *want* it to double. You want enough of those yeast cells to still have the energy to keep raising that dough once it's in the oven.

I like to bake this bread at 475°F (246°C). If your bread is in a loaf pan, and assuming your oven thermostat is accurate, it will take 40

FIGURE 8.5. Scoring the dough just before baking.

TIP

If you want to add steam to the baking process, review the suggestions on pages 55–56. For now, just concentrate on getting comfortable with the basic shaping, proofing, and baking processes.

to 45 minutes to bake. Free-form loaves baked directly on the baking stone might take a few minutes less. You will have to make a few test runs to see what works best with your oven, but most 500-gram loaves should bake nicely within, say, 35 to 50 minutes at this temperature.

I use a wooden pizza peel for getting my bread in and out of the oven. It may not be traditional, but I much prefer putting a piece of parchment paper on the peel first. It makes it so much easier to slide the bread off the peel and onto the baking stone! (If you don't have a peel, you can use a rimless baking sheet.) Take your proofing basket or bowl (plastic wrap off), and quickly tip the bowl over to turn the dough onto the peel. If you want to slash it, now is the time. I like a serrated bread knife for this; quickly and confidently make 2 or 3 slash marks on your loaf. ¼" to ½" is the depth to aim for. It's important to get the dough in the oven promptly, so don't spend a lot of time on slashing.

Using a jerking motion with the peel, slide the dough off the parchment paper and onto your baking stone; quickly shut the oven door. Set your timer for 35 minutes, and take a break. Resist the temptation to open the oven door until the timer goes off.

Check the bread after 35 minutes. It will have risen nicely and should be at least starting to brown. You will probably want to bake it a few more minutes; if you slashed the dough, the edges of the slash marks will be getting darker now and may even look almost black. That's a good time to take it out of the oven. Use your peel again for this, helping the bread onto the peel with tongs or a wooden spoon if needed. Put your beautiful loaf onto a cooling rack, stand back and admire it. Please let it cool for at least 45 minutes, preferably an hour, before you cut into it. (I force myself to do dishes and clean up the kitchen at this point; if that doesn't take enough time, there's always a *New York Times* crossword somewhere.)

It seems like there was a lot of detail here for just one simple loaf of bread. I can tell you from my own experience that it won't be long before this will all seem like second nature. You have made a loaf of bread with your own hands! If you never thought of yourself as a bread baker before today, well, now you *are* a bread baker. Enjoy this moment. Be proud of yourself.

Variation: Long-fermented No-knead Bread

This method gives you the advantages of long-fermented sourdough bread, with the convenience of no-knead yeast bread. This also allows you a lot more flexibility in fitting bread-making into your schedule; once you've mixed up your dough, you simply set it aside for 8 to 12 hours, or even more, before shaping and proofing it.

It's quite simple: Just **decrease the amount of yeast to 0.75 g (¼ teaspoon)**. The smaller amount of yeast results in a slower rise, which allows for more flavor development. Plus you can just mix it up in the morning, go off for your day's work, and finish it in the evening. Or mix it at night and bake it first thing in the morning. And remember, if you want to slow down the process even more, you can simply pop the dough bucket into the fridge at any point after the dough is mixed. Take it out 2 to 3 hours ahead of when you want to shape and proof it, to allow it to come back to room temperature. Then proceed as usual with shaping.

Bagels and Other Specialty Yeast Breads

Montreal-style Bagels

This recipe is adapted from one in *Artisan Breads in 5 Minutes a Day* (see Appendix B). This dough is a little less sweet than the original, but it has a marvelous flavor from the malt powder and honey. Montreal bagels are traditionally baked in a wood-fired oven, but they are quite delicious baked in your kitchen oven on a baking stone. They are usually coated on both sides with sesame seeds after boiling, but I find it easier to just sprinkle the seeds on top. These bagels are softer and not so dense as classic New York-style bagels, and they make the most delicious sandwiches. My favorite bagel sandwich is sharp cheddar cheese with thin slices of onion and tomato; the bagels are so moist and flavorful, condiments would be redundant. And, of course, they are fabulous toasted, with cream cheese and homemade jam.

Timing

- 5 minutes to measure ingredients and mix dough
- 20 minutes for autolyze phase
- 2 to 3 hours to ferment dough
- 30 minutes to shape dough
- 10 to 15 minutes to boil bagels
- 20 to 25 minutes to bake

SEXY SCIENCE TALK

Why Are Bagels Boiled Before Baking?

The boiling phase of bagel recipes intimidated me for the longest time, probably because I didn't understand why it was necessary; the recipes never explained. The main purpose of the brief dunking in the boiling pot is to gelatinize the starches on the outside of the bagel prior to baking. This results in a smooth, thin, shiny crust. What goes into the boiling pot varies depending on the type of bagel. For New York-style bagels, the boiling pot often has just water and either baking soda or cream of tartar; in the recipe for Montreal-style bagels below, the boiling pot has honey and malt powder. Whichever kind you choose to make, don't be put off by the boiling phase. It's quite easy and really does make a difference.

Equipment you'll definitely need

- Large mixing bowl (stainless steel, glass, Pyrex, or ceramic)
- Wooden spoon
- 6-quart stainless steel pot for boiling
- Slotted spoon
- Large cutting board
- Dough scraper or bread knife for dividing dough

Stuff that's not absolutely necessary but recommended

- Kitchen scale
- 2-quart dough-rising bucket
- Parchment paper
- Baking stone
- Pizza peel or rimless cookie sheet

Ingredients	Metric	US	Baker's %
• Unchlorinated water, warm	350 g	1½ cups	70
• SAF or other instant yeast	4 g	1 tsp	1
• Malt powder	25 g	3 Tbsp	5
• Honey	43 g	2 Tbsp	8.6
• Egg, large (optional)		1	
• Sea salt	10 g	1½ tsp	2
• Unbleached bread flour	400 g	about 3 cups	80
• Whole-wheat flour, preferably stone-ground	100 g	about ¾ cup	20
• Honey (for boiling pot)	43 g	2 Tbsp	
• Malt powder (for boiling pot)	16 g	2 Tbsp	
• Sesame seeds for coating bagels			

TIP

At this point, you may refrigerate the dough; be sure it is covered so it won't dry out. It will keep for at least a week. This dough is fairly soft, so it can be a bit easier to work with and shape when it's cold.

Mixing and Fermenting the Dough

In a large mixing bowl, blend the warm water, yeast, malt powder, honey, egg (if using), and salt until yeast and salt are dissolved. Stir in the flours just until blended, then let dough rest for about 20 minutes. Stir for 2 or 3 more minutes.

FIGURE 9.1. Preshape bagels by dividing dough and forming it into balls.

FIGURE 9.2. Bagel dough formed into rings prior to boiling.

Cover the bowl or put the dough into a 2-quart dough-rising bucket. Let it ferment at room temperature until the dough doubles in volume or fills the bucket, about 2 to 3 hours. The dough may flatten out a bit or collapse in on itself; don't worry—this is normal.

FIGURE 9.3. Bagels in boiling pot.

Shaping, Boiling, and Baking the Bagels

Put your baking stone on a rack in the middle of your oven. Preheat the oven to 400°F (204°C). Turn the dough out onto a floured board and divide into 12 pieces. Shape each piece into a ball, dusting with more flour if needed. Cover the balls with plastic wrap and let rest about 20 minutes.

In your saucepan or stockpot, bring to a boil 4 quarts of water. Reduce heat to low and add 43 g (2 tablespoons) honey and 16 g (2 tablespoons) malt powder, stirring to dissolve.

Form the bagels by poking a hole in each dough ball with your thumb. Use your fingers to gently stretch open the hole, shaping the dough into a ring about 3" to 4" in diameter. I like to shape all the bagels at once, then do all the boiling at once; it just seems a little less hectic to me.

Have ready a pizza peel or rimless cookie sheet with a piece of parchment paper on it. Drop bagels into the simmering water a few at a time, making sure they aren't too crowded. In my 6-quart saucepan, I usually do 3 bagels at a time. Let them simmer for 1 minute, then flip them over with your slotted spoon and simmer another 30 seconds on the other side. Lift out of the boiling pot and onto the parchment paper. Quickly, while the bagels are still moist, generously dust them with sesame seeds. Be sure to space the bagels at least an inch apart.

Continue boiling bagels until your peel or cookie sheet is full. Quickly slide the bagels onto your baking stone and bake for 20 to 25 minutes. They will puff up and turn a beautiful golden brown. Transfer to a cooling rack. Let cool at least a few minutes before eating.

FIGURE 9.4. Dusting bagels with sesame seeds just before baking.

Variation: Bialys

To make bialys, follow the recipe for Montreal-style bagels up to the point of forming the dough into balls. Let the dough rest 15 to 20 minutes, and preheat your oven and baking stone to 450°F (232°C).

While the dough balls are resting, sauté ½ medium onion, finely chopped, in 14 g (1 tablespoon) peanut oil or canola oil over medium-low heat; the onion should be translucent, not brown and crispy. Stir in 2 to 3 g (¾ to 1 teaspoon) poppy seeds, and season to taste with salt and pepper.

We like to add some finely chopped garlic to the onion and sometimes throw in some sesame seeds along with the poppy seeds. Not strictly traditional, but quite yummy.

FIGURE 9.5. Finished bagels on cooling rack.

FIGURE 9.6. Bialys ready to bake.

Have ready a pizza peel or rimless cookie sheet with a piece of parchment paper on it.

Flatten out each dough ball by forming a depression in the middle with your thumbs. You should have a round 3" to 4" in diameter with a thick rim and fairly thin center. Fill the depression with a spoonful of the onion-poppy seed mixture. Use the back of the spoon to press the mixture into each bialy on the parchment paper as it is formed. When the parchment is full, slide bialys quickly onto the hot baking stone and bake for about 12 minutes or until they are golden brown and puffy. Be careful not to overbake. Transfer to a cooling rack and cool for a few minutes before eating.

 ## English Muffins (makes 12)

English muffins and crumpets were originally made using a beer barm (see Chapter 14 for more about barm) but today are usually made with commercial yeast. Crumpet rings are helpful, but I've had very good results with English muffins without rings; I just carefully pat the dough into flattish circles. They may not be perfectly round, but they're delicious all the same.

Timing

- 5 to 10 minutes to measure ingredients and mix and knead dough
- 4 to 5 hours to ferment dough
- 15 to 20 minutes to shape dough
- 30 minutes to proof dough
- 20 to 25 minutes to bake

Equipment you'll definitely need

- Large mixing bowl (stainless steel, glass, Pyrex, or ceramic)
- Wooden spoon
- Smaller bowl of cool water for dipping into
- Large cutting board
- Dough scraper or bread knife for dividing dough
- Griddle or large cast-iron skillet

Stuff that's not absolutely necessary but recommended

- Kitchen scale
- 2-quart dough-rising bucket
- Crumpet rings (King Arthur Flour sells sets; substitute tuna cans with both ends removed)

Ingredients	Metric	US	Baker's %
• Unchlorinated water, warm	236 g	1 cup	52
• SAF or other instant yeast	4 g	1 tsp	0.8
• Unchlorinated water, cool	118 g	½ cup	26
• All-purpose or pastry flour	450 g	3½ cups	100
• Sea salt	10 g	1½ tsp	2.2

Mixing the Dough

Dissolve the yeast in the warm water in a mixing bowl. Add the cool water, flour, and salt. Mix with a spoon just until well blended. Turn dough out onto a floured board. Dip your hand in the small bowl of water and knead the dough for about 3 minutes. Dip your hand in water whenever dough starts to stick.

Fermenting the Dough

Put the muffin dough back in the mixing bowl and cover with a clean dish towel, or in a 2-quart dough-rising bucket and put on the lid. Let the dough ferment at room temperature for 2 hours, then move it to a warm spot, ideally 78°F (25°C), for another 2 to 3 hours. If you don't have somewhere that warm to ferment the batter, just allow more fermentation time. Dough will double in volume; in the dough-rising bucket, the dough will nearly fill the bucket when fully fermented.

Shaping the Dough

Gently deflate the dough and turn it out onto a floured board. Divide the dough into 12 equal pieces. Shape each piece into a ball, then flatten into rounds about ¾" thick, and about 3¼" in diameter. If using crumpet rings, butter them and dust lightly with flour, and place the flattened rounds in the rings. Cover the rounds with a floured dish towel, and let rest in a warm place for about 30 minutes.

Baking the Muffins

Heat the griddle to about 400°F (204°C); at the correct heat, a drop of water will sizzle on the griddle surface but not explode. Oil the griddle lightly, and put as many crumpet rings on the griddle as will fit without crowding. Place the muffins on the griddle, and bake 7 to 10 minutes on the first side, then turn and bake another 7 to 10 minutes. Muffins are done when lightly browned on both sides. Let cool on a wire rack before eating.

Crumpets (makes 12)

Timing

- 5 minutes to measure ingredients and mix dough
- 4 to 5 hours to ferment dough
- 30 minutes to shape dough
- 6 to 8 minutes to bake

Equipment you'll definitely need

- Large mixing bowl (stainless steel, glass, Pyrex, or ceramic)
- Whisk
- Crumpet rings (King Arthur Flour sells sets; substitute tuna cans with both ends removed)
- Griddle or large cast-iron skillet

Stuff that's not absolutely necessary but recommended

- Kitchen scale

Ingredients	Metric	US	Baker's %
• Unchlorinated water, warm	350 g	1½ cups	127
• Milk, warmed to 110ºF (43ºC)	230 g	1 cup	84
• SAF or other instant yeast	4 g	1 tsp	1.4
• All-purpose or pastry flour	275 g	2 cups	100
• Egg, large, beaten	56 g	1	20
• Sea salt	3.5 g	½ tsp	1.2

Mixing the Batter

Dissolve the yeast in the warm water in a mixing bowl. Add the warmed milk, flour, beaten egg, and salt. Mix, using the whisk, until the batter is smooth and the consistency of heavy cream. Cover the bowl with plastic wrap.

Fermenting the Batter

Let the crumpet batter ferment at room temperature for 2 hours, then move it to a warm spot, ideally 78°F (25°C) for another 2 to 3 hours. If you don't have somewhere that warm to ferment the batter, just allow more fermentation time. The batter is ready to bake when it is full of bubbles.

Baking the Crumpets

Butter the crumpet rings and dust lightly with flour. Heat the griddle to about 400°F (204°C); at the correct heat, a drop of water will sizzle on the griddle surface but not explode. Oil the griddle lightly, and put as many crumpet rings on the griddle as will fit without crowding. Pour the crumpet batter into each ring to about ½" (1 cm) deep. The bubbles in the batter will start to break open as the crumpets cook. When the tops of the crumpets are set, in about 4 to 6 minutes, lift off the rings, turn the crumpets, and cook another 1 to 2 minutes. Remove from the griddle, and serve warm, or cool on a wire rack.

Comfort Zone 2: Kneaded Breads

If you've been happy with the bread you've made using the no-knead technique, you may be wondering why anyone would bother ever kneading their bread dough. As you now know, even without kneading, there is sufficient gluten development in the dough to make good bread. I suspect—and certainly hope—that once you go through the no-knead process a few times, you will be thoroughly bitten by the baking bug and decide to try hand-kneading your dough.

You're stepping out of your initial comfort zone; why not make a party out of it? Invite a few friends over; mix up a couple batches of no-knead bread; then spend just a few minutes kneading one batch. Observe, and make notes if you wish, what differences you see as the dough rises, how it feels in your hands when you shape it, how it bakes, and what the finished bread is like. You may decide that no-knead bread is just fine for you, and that's entirely up to you. Or, you may choose to knead some breads and not others. Either way, you will be making wonderful bread!

Hand-kneaded Challah

Timing

- 3 to 5 minutes to measure ingredients and mix dough
- 20 minutes for autolyze phase
- 8 to 12 minutes to knead
- 1 to 2 hours to ferment dough
- 10 minutes to divide and braid dough
- Up to 1 hour to proof dough
- 30 to 40 minutes to bake

Equipment you'll definitely need

- Large mixing bowl (stainless steel, glass, Pyrex, or ceramic)
- Wooden spoon
- Large cutting board for shaping dough
- Pizza peel or rimless baking sheet
- Parchment paper
- Pastry brush

Stuff that's not absolutely necessary but recommended

- Kitchen scale
- 2-quart dough-rising bucket

Ingredients	Metric	US	Baker's %
• Unchlorinated water, lukewarm	350 g	1½ cups	70
• SAF or other instant yeast	4 g	1 tsp	1
• Unbleached bread flour	350 g	about 2½ cups	70
• Whole wheat flour, preferably stone-ground	150 g	about 1⅓ cups	30
• Extra-virgin olive oil	20 g	2 Tbsp	4
• Egg yolk, beaten lightly	about 95 g	2 chicken (or 1 duck)	
• Sea salt	10 g	1½ tsps	2
• Egg, lightly beaten, for brushing		2 yolks or 1 whole egg	
• Sesame seeds (optional)	20 to 30 g	2 to 3 Tbsp	

Mixing the Dough

Stir the yeast into the warm water. Add the olive oil and beaten egg yolks. Blend in the whole wheat flour and bread flour, stirring to moisten all the flour. Let dough rest for 15 to 20 minutes before kneading. Stir in the salt just before kneading.

Kneading the Dough

Knead the dough for a total of 8 to 12 minutes. I recommend kneading for half the total time, then letting the dough rest for about 10 minutes before completing the kneading. The dough will be fairly smooth and springy.

Fermenting the Dough

Cover the mixing bowl with plastic wrap, or put the dough into your dough-rising bucket and put the lid on. Let it ferment at room temperature for 1 to 2 hours; it will fill up the dough-rising bucket when it is ready to shape.

Dividing, Shaping, and Proofing the Dough

Gently deflate the dough and turn it out onto a lightly floured board. Divide the dough into 3 or 4 pieces, depending on which type of braid you plan to do. The classic 3-way braid is easiest, although the 4-way braid is more authentic. (I found a very good video on YouTube demonstrating the 4-way braid that made it very easy to learn.)

Gently roll each piece into a log about 12" to 15" long. Try not to handle the dough any more than necessary while shaping. I like to put a piece of parchment paper on my peel and braid the loaf on the parchment; this helps avoid over-handling. Braid the pieces into a loaf, sealing the ends of the logs together to form the ends of the loaf. Cover the braided loaf loosely with plastic wrap and let proof at room temperature for up to an hour while the oven preheats.

Preheat the oven, with your baking stone on a middle rack, to 475°F (246°C); the stone needs at least 45 minutes to thoroughly heat. (If you're not using a baking stone, preheat the oven to 400°F (204°C) for at least 15 minutes.)

Baking the Challah

Turn the heat in the oven down to 400°F (204°C). Uncover the challah. Using a pastry brush, lightly brush the beaten egg over the surface of the loaf. Sprinkle on the sesame seeds, if you are using them. If you're using a baking stone, use the peel to slide the loaf, parchment paper and all, quickly onto the stone. If using a baking sheet, slip the baking sheet under the parchment paper and slide the sheet into the oven.

Bake the loaf for 30 to 40 minutes. The egg wash will turn the crust a lovely, slightly shiny, dark golden brown. Remove carefully from the oven, using your peel. Cool the challah on a rack.

Variations on Basic Kneaded Bread

I bet you'll be surprised how quickly you will start thinking of items to add to your bread dough, even when you are still new to baking. My mother used to add leftover cooked cereals to the bread dough, and it usually turned out really well. From what I know now, I'm guessing

FIGURE 10.1. Baked challah.

the times it didn't come out quite so well, it had something to do with the proportion of cereal added. That is, if too much non-gluten cereal, such as oatmeal, is mixed in, it might compromise the gluten structure by essentially diluting the gluten's stretchiness, thus affecting the rise and texture of the bread. The results aren't always the prettiest, but it hardly ever happens that the bread you make is actually not good to eat. I promise you, after all these years, I'm still learning, and I hope that never changes.

Adding Seeds and Nuts to Bread Dough

I love making bread with lots of seeds. Seeds and nuts add crunch to the texture of bread as well as nutrition and a pleasing visual interest. The main thing to know about adding seeds, nuts, or dried fruit to bread is that they absorb moisture from the dough, unless you soak them ahead of time for at least several hours. For yeast bread, I suggest putting them to soak in the morning, if you plan to bake later in the day; or soak them overnight, if you plan to bake in the morning. You millennials will probably have an app on your smartphones to keep track of your seed-soaking schedule, but I'm a simple girl; I like the morning/evening thing. When I make sourdough or other long-fermented bread, I just get the seeds soaking when I refresh the starter; that way I know the seeds have been soaking for at least 8 hours by the time I mix up my dough.

Any time you add another grain to the dough, such as oatmeal or grits, be aware that the hydration level of the dough will change. If the grain added is dry, it will absorb some of the moisture in the dough; if it is wet, as in cooked cereal, it will make the dough slightly softer. It takes time to get used to handling wet soft dough, so you might find that refrigerating it before shaping is beneficial.

Here's one of my favorite recipes using several kinds of seeds. It's similar to the challah recipe above but without the egg.

Seeded and Kneaded Yeast Bread

Timing

- 8 to 12 hours to soak seeds
- 3 to 5 minutes to measure ingredients and mix dough
- 20 minutes for autolyze phase
- 8 to 12 minutes to knead
- 1 to 2 hours to ferment dough
- 1 hour to proof dough
- 35 to 45 minutes to bake

Equipment you'll definitely need

- Small bowl for soaking seeds
- Large mixing bowl (stainless steel, glass, Pyrex, or ceramic)
- Wooden spoon
- Large cutting board for shaping dough
- Pizza peel or rimless baking sheet
- Parchment paper

Stuff that's not absolutely necessary but recommended

- Kitchen scale
- 2-quart dough-rising bucket

Ingredients	Metric	US	Baker's %
• Sesame seeds, raw	50 g	⅓ cup	10
• Sunflower seeds, raw, unsalted	65 g	½ cup	13
• Flax seeds	25 g	2 Tbsp	5
• Tap water, room temperature	175 g	¾ cup	35
• Unchlorinated water, lukewarm	350 g	1½ cups	70
• SAF or other instant yeast	4 g	1 tsp	1
• Extra-virgin olive oil	20 g	2 Tbsp	4
• Unbleached bread flour	350 g	about 2½ cups	70
• Whole wheat flour, preferably stone-ground	150 g	about 1⅓ cups	30
• Sea salt	10 g	1½ tsp	2

Soaking the Seeds

In a small bowl, cover the seeds with tap water. The amount of water isn't critical; the important thing is to make sure all the seeds are completely covered. Let them soak for at least 8 hours. At the end of the soaking time, if there is any excess water, drain it off before mixing the seeds into the dough.

Mixing the Dough

In a large mixing bowl, stir the yeast into the lukewarm water. Add the olive oil, then the bread flour and whole wheat flour, stirring to blend. Let dough rest for 15 to 20 minutes; then add the salt.

Kneading the Dough

Knead the dough for a total of 8 to 12 minutes. I recommend kneading for half the total time, then letting the dough rest for about 10 minutes before completing the kneading. The dough will be fairly smooth and springy.

Fermenting the Dough

Cover the mixing bowl with plastic wrap, or put the dough into your dough-rising bucket and put the lid on. Let it ferment at room temperature for 1 to 2 hours; it will fill up the dough-rising bucket when it is ready to shape.

Shaping and Proofing the Dough

Gently deflate the dough and turn it out onto a lightly floured board. Gently shape it into a round or oblong loaf; try not to handle the dough any more than necessary while shaping. Put the loaf in a banneton or other proofing basket, seam side up, or in a greased standard loaf pan (seam side down). Cover the loaf loosely with plastic wrap and let proof at room temperature for up to 1 hour while the oven preheats.

Preheat the oven, with your baking stone on a middle rack, to 475°F (246°C); the stone needs at least 45 minutes to thoroughly heat. If you're not using a baking stone, preheat the oven to 425°F (218°C) for at least 15 minutes; preheat to 400°F (204°C) if using a glass or Pyrex loaf pan.

Baking the Bread

If you're using a baking stone, put parchment paper on your peel and tip the dough from the proofing basket onto the parchment. Quickly slash the top of the loaf, use the peel to slide the loaf, parchment paper and all, onto the stone. If using a baking sheet, slip the baking sheet under the parchment paper and slide the sheet into the oven.

Bake the loaf for 30 to 40 minutes. Remove carefully from the oven using your peel or oven mitts. Cool the bread for at least 1 hour on a rack before cutting.

Unusual Yeast Breads

 ALL RIGHT, so coffee cake and baba au rhum aren't typical breads. But they are both raised with yeast, and I'm including them because, well, it's my book and I want to.

Mum's Coffee Cake

When I was young, my mum used to make this wonderful coffee cake every so often. This was a yeast bread dough, rolled out, and covered with melted butter, brown sugar, cinnamon, and raisins. The whole thing was then rolled up into a long fat tube, formed into a circle, snipped to expose the filling (see photos), and baked. While still warm from the oven, it was drizzled with a confectioner's sugar icing. It was large and impressive and so delicious.

These days, I like to use the Montreal-style bagel dough (see Chapter 9) to make this coffee cake; the slight sweetening from honey and malt powder make this extra good. However, since most recipes in this book are based on 500 grams of flour, you can easily substitute another bread recipe if you prefer. Add chopped pecans or other nuts if you wish, along with the other filling ingredients.

The instructions below assume you have already made and fermented the bread dough you want to use. The dough is easier to roll out when it is cold, so it's good if you can make it the day before you plan to bake.

FIGURE 11.1. Mum's coffee cake, iced, warm, and ready to eat.

Timing

- 3 to 5 minutes to roll out dough
- 5 minutes to melt butter and add filling ingredients
- 5 minutes to roll up, shape, and snip coffee cake
- 1 to 2 hours to proof coffee cake
- 35 to 45 minutes to bake

Equipment you'll definitely need

- Large cutting board for shaping coffee cake
- Rolling pin
- Pastry brush
- Large baking sheet or jelly roll pan
- Parchment paper
- Wire whisk

Stuff that's not absolutely necessary but recommended

- Baking stone large enough for the coffee cake
- Pizza peel or large rimless cookie sheet

Ingredients	Metric	US
• Montreal-style bagel dough (see Chapter 9)		1 batch
• Unsalted butter, melted	113 g	½ cup (1 stick)
• Light brown sugar, packed	220 g	1 cup (or more to taste)
• Cinnamon, ground	6 g	2 tsp
• Seedless raisins or currants	300 g	2 cups
• Pecans or walnuts, chopped (optional)	about 110 g	½ cup
• Confectioner's sugar	128 g	1 cup
• Milk or cream	15 to 30 g	1 to 2 Tbsp
• Vanilla extract	2 g	½ tsp

Preparing the Dough and Filling

Turn the dough out onto a large, floured cutting board. Roll out the dough to a large oblong about ½" thick. Transfer to a piece of parchment paper, turning it so one long side is facing you. Let the dough rest while you prepare the filling.

Melt the butter over low heat in a small saucepan or in the microwave. In a small bowl, mix together the brown sugar and cinnamon. Measure the raisins and separate them so there are no clumps.

Using the pastry brush, spread the melted butter over the whole surface of the dough. Sprinkle on the brown sugar-cinnamon mixture, then the raisins or currants and nuts (if using).

FIGURE 11.2. Dough rolled out with toppings.

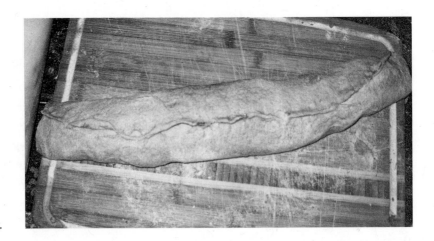

FIGURE 11.3. Forming the dough into a log.

FIGURE 11.4. The log is formed into a ring.

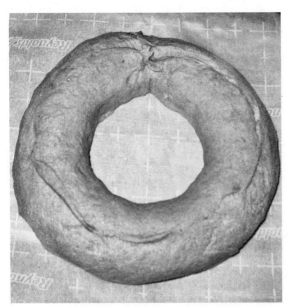

Shaping and Snipping the Coffee Cake

Starting on the long side facing you, carefully roll up the dough; you will have a long log 3" to 4" thick. Seal the other long edge of the dough to the cylinder by pinching it together with your fingers (Figure 11.3). Take the ends of the log and bring them together, again pinching the dough to seal, to form a large ring (Figure 11.4).

Using kitchen shears, make a series of snips across the log, about 1½" apart, cutting about three-quarters of the way through (Figure 11.5). Go all the way around the circle, adjusting the width of the sections if needed so it comes out fairly evenly. Then turn each section to the right, so that it lies at about a 45-degree angle, exposing the filling (Figure 11.6). Each piece will lie slightly over the adjacent piece.

Proofing the Dough

Cover the coffee cake loosely with plastic wrap, and let proof at room temperature for 1 to 2 hours. (If the dough was not chilled before using, proof for about 1 hour.) It will not double in volume, but the dough will look soft and puffy.

Baking the Coffee Cake

Preheat your oven to 350°F (176°C). If you're using a baking stone, start preheating the oven, with the baking stone on a rack in the middle, about an hour before you plan to bake. Otherwise, preheat for at least 15 minutes.

Using the pizza peel or cookie sheet, quickly slide the coffee cake, parchment paper and all, onto the baking stone. (If you're not using a baking stone, just leave it on the cookie sheet.) Bake for 35 to 45 minutes; coffee cake will be golden brown all over. Transfer to a cooling rack, still on the parchment paper.

Icing

Mix together the milk or cream and vanilla extract. Using a whisk, blend with the confectioner's sugar a little at a time, until smooth and creamy; it might seem a little thin, but it will thicken as it sets. Add a little more milk or cream if needed. Drizzle the icing over the coffee cake while it is still warm. Cool until the icing has set, then carefully lift the coffee cake off the parchment paper. Enjoy the coffee cake warm or at room temperature. Store in an airtight plastic bag or container when it is completely cooled.

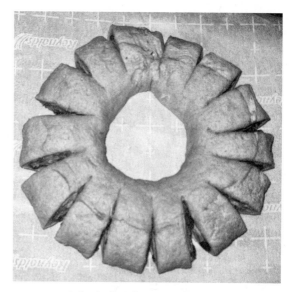

FIGURE 11.5. Snip the log about ¾ through...

FIGURE 11.6. ...then turn the dough sections to expose the filling and form a pinwheel.

Baba au Rhum

This is David's favorite cake; I make it every year for his birthday in March. Although it is leavened with yeast and has a fairly lengthy fermentation time, it is more of a cake than a bread; after baking, it is soaked with a rum-laced sugar syrup. It is well worth the effort and time it takes to make.

David and I have been to Paris, France together three times. We stayed at the same hotel every time, the Hotel Amélie in the Seventh Arrondissement, on the quiet residential Rue Amélie, just off the busier Rue St. Dominique. Around the corner from the hotel is a wonderful little patisserie: I don't recall the name, but every day the shop window displayed the Gateau du Jour (cake of the day). David was enamored of this patisserie from the first time the Gateau du Jour was Baba au Rhum.

From then on, every day we would pass the shop, checking out the Gateau du Jour. David doesn't let language barriers worry him much; he knows enough to say "bonjour" when entering a shop and "au revoir" when leaving, and "Gateau du Jour" is just about the only other French phrase he has bothered to master. The lovely middle-aged French ladies behind the patisserie counter would see him looking at the window display, and by the time we went in, they were all smiles. They would sometimes even anticipate him and have the Gateau du Jour already in a little box for him. He just smiled, laughed, and talked to them, mostly in English, but it didn't matter. He was polite, charming, and clearly appreciated their art. I think the women looked forward to his visits, and we certainly look forward to baba au rhum every March.

Baba au rhum is traditionally baked in a fluted tube pan. I like to use a 9" by 13" baking pan instead.

Timing

- 1 to 1½ hours to make and ferment sponge
- 10 to 15 minutes to make batter

- 1½ to 3 hours to ferment baba
- 50 to 60 minutes to bake
- 5 minutes to prepare rum syrup

Equipment you'll definitely need

- Medium-sized mixing bowl
- Large mixing bowl (stainless steel, glass, Pyrex, or ceramic) or stand mixer with large bowl
- Wooden spoon, if not using a mixer
- Large cutting board for shaping cake
- Fluted tube pan or 9" by 13" baking pan

Stuff that's not absolutely necessary but recommended

- Wire whisk
- Rolling pin
- Kitchen shears for snipping dough
- Baking stone large enough for the cake
- Pizza peel or large rimless cookie sheet

Ingredients	Metric	US	Baker's %
• All-purpose flour	550 g	about 4¼ cups	100
• Milk	230 g	1 cup	42
• SAF or other instant yeast	12 g	4 tsp	2.1
• Butter	227 g	1 cup	41
• Granulated sugar	150 g	¾ cup	27
• Eggs, large	280 g	5	51
• Sea salt	5 g	1 tsp	0.9
• Lemon rind, freshly grated		1 tsp	
• Seedless raisins or currants	150 g	1 cup	27
• Blanched almonds, thinly sliced	65 g	½ cup	12
• Rum syrup			
• Granulated sugar	300 g	1½ cups	
• Water	710 g	3 cups	
• Dark rum	180 g	¾ cup or more to taste	

Making the Sponge

Scald the milk and let it cool to lukewarm, 105° to 115°F (40° to 46°C). Put the yeast in a medium mixing bowl, and pour the cooled milk over the yeast, stirring to dissolve. Using a whisk or wooden spoon, beat in 128 g (1 cup) of the flour until well-blended. Cover the bowl with plastic wrap, and let ferment in a warm spot until the sponge has just about doubled in volume.

Mixing the Batter

In a large mixing bowl, beat the butter until soft. Gradually add the sugar, mixing until light and creamy. Beat in the eggs, one at a time.

FIGURE 11.7. Currant-rich baba au rhum.

Add the sponge, the rest of the flour, the salt, lemon rind, and raisins or currants. Stir the batter vigorously until it is smooth and stretchy, about 5 minutes.

Fermenting the Baba

Grease the tube pan or baking pan. Spread the sliced almonds over the bottom of the pan. Spread the batter on top of the almonds. Cover pan with plastic wrap. Let the baba ferment until nearly doubled in volume; it will almost fill the baking pan when it's ready. In a warm spot, this won't take much more than an hour; it has quite a lot of yeast. (I like to mix this batter in the morning and let it ferment in a cool spot most of the day before baking; as with other breads, the longer fermentation time improves the flavor.)

Baking and Finishing the Baba

Preheat the oven to 350°F (176°C). Bake the baba for 50 to 60 minutes. The top and sides will be golden brown. Transfer pan to cooling rack, but leave the baba in the pan for now.

Rum syrup: Bring the sugar and water to a boil, stirring to dissolve the sugar. As soon as it is dissolved, remove from the heat and stir in the rum. Immediately pour the syrup over the cake, taking your time so it soaks in without splashing over the sides of the pan. If it doesn't seem to be soaking in fairly quickly, pour on some of the syrup, then wait for a few minutes before adding the rest.

Baba au rhum is delicious on its own or with heavy cream or vanilla ice cream.

PART THREE

BREADS MADE WITH PRE-FERMENTS

Comfort Zone 3: Sponge, Poolish, Biga

IF MAKING AND MAINTAINING a storage leaven like sourdough starter is out of your comfort zone, try using a *pre-ferment*. This is a lot like a sourdough starter, with two important distinctions: It is usually made with commercial yeast; and it is most often made within hours of when you mix up your bread dough. For most of my breads, the pre-ferment would be mixed 9 to 16 hours before I plan to mix my dough. It is amazing how much flavor this adds to even plain white bread. Many of the white breads of Italy are made with a pre-ferment called *biga*; in France the sponge-like pre-ferment is called *poolish*. What's the difference between them? After all, the purpose is basically the same: to raise bread dough.

The Italian biga is the stiffest of these pre-ferments. Italian bakers, especially in northern Italy, where the flour milled from local wheat tends to have less protein and gluten-forming potential, use a fairly high proportion of biga in their dough to increase the rising ability and structure of the bread.

The French poolish, which is essentially the same thing as a sponge, usually accounts for less than half the volume of dough recipes. However, most modern recipes using a sponge ferment the sponge for only 1 or 2 hours before mixing the bread dough; poolish, by contrast, is generally fermented 4 to 6 hours, which is long enough to begin developing enough character to benefit the flavor of the bread.

So which pre-ferment should you use for which kind of bread? That is up to you, although your choice might be determined by your schedule or what kind of bread you plan to make. For example, if you have plenty of time and are going to make Italian ciabatta or another white bread, the long-fermenting biga is an excellent choice. Whole-grain

FIGURE 12.1. Biga just mixed up.

FIGURE 12.2. Biga after fermentation, ready to use in dough.

breads often benefit from a sponge or poolish made even a couple of hours ahead of time. Try using different flours in the pre-ferment, keeping in mind that it's a good idea to use unbleached bread flour for at least half the total. The sponge is also a good choice when making rustic breads and pizzas. Have fun and experiment!

Master Recipe: Italian Biga

Ingredients	Metric	US	Baker's %
• SAF or other instant yeast	0.75 g	¼ tsp	2.5
• Unchlorinated water, warm	60 g	¼ cup	20
• Unchlorinated water, room temperature	200 g	¾ cup + 4 tsp	67
• Unbleached bread flour or all-purpose flour	300 g	about 2¼ cups	100

Stir yeast into warm water to dissolve. Add the remaining water and flour, stirring for 2 to 3 minutes. Cover and let rise 6 to 24 hours in a cool spot. Use right away or store in refrigerator up to 5 days.

Simplified Method: Sponge or Poolish

Essentially, when you make a sponge, you are building your bread dough in two stages. You can make a fairly large quantity of sponge and use it at different times to make bread, but I feel that this makes the most sense if you are baking at least a few loaves over several days. If you have a bake sale coming up or are baking for a big dinner party, go for it. Here's a simpler way to take advantage of the benefits of a sponge, with no worries about using it up promptly: Mix your yeasted bread dough as usual, *except* use only half the total amount of flour. Make sure your mixing bowl is large enough to allow for the sponge to expand.

TIP

If making whole-grain bread, use at least half of the recipe's whole-grain flour in the sponge. The texture of the bread will improve because of the effects of fermentation, and the bran and germ in the grain will be appreciated by the hungry yeast.

Stir the sponge for at least 1 minute to hydrate the flour and blend thoroughly. Cover the bowl loosely with plastic wrap, and leave to ferment at room temperature for at least 1 hour. The sponge will expand, but because it is so wet, it will rise only so far before it collapses on itself. By then it will be bubbly and fragrant and ready to mix into your dough.

At this point, just add the remaining flour in your recipe, along with the salt. Knead, ferment, and bake the bread according to your recipe's directions.

Variation: Poolish

As mentioned above, the main difference between a sponge and poolish is that the latter has a longer fermentation period. To slow the fermentation, it's necessary to cut the yeast down to a tiny amount. Refrigerating it will, of course, also slow down the fermentation. Keep in mind that you'll want to use up the poolish within 3 or 4 days; after that, the yeast cells will start to die off and can create some "off" flavors.

To make your poolish, simply follow the sponge method above, but cut the yeast down to no more than 0.75 g (¼ teaspoon).

Making Bread with Pre-ferments

France and Italy are both well-known for their many delicious breads. If you venture outside the big cities and visit small artisan bakeries, you'll discover a wide variety of regional specialties, breads that are often made with some kind of pre-ferment like biga or poolish. Here's a ciabatta recipe and variation, to help you get into the groove of using a pre-ferment.

TIP

If you can't use up all your sponge or poolish in a few days, you can freeze the extra until you're ready to make more bread. It's best to freeze it within a day of starting it, though; the longer it ferments, the less stable it can be after being frozen. Thaw gradually in the refrigerator for at least 24 hours, then take out of the fridge about 1 hour before mixing up your dough.

Ciabatta

Ciabatta, like the Roman-style pizza (Chapter 13), is made with a very wet dough and can be challenging for the home baker. This high hydration level results in a very light, bubbly crust and a shiny, tender crumb, but it also makes kneading difficult. If you're not used to working with very wet doughs, I recommend kneading it using a heavy mixer like a KitchenAid, with a dough hook. If you don't have such a mixer (I don't), follow the directions below for hand-kneading.

Ciabatta is the first bread I ever made using a pre-ferment. I remember being fairly astounded at how much flavor the bread had, considering it was made with 100% white flour. Almost every time I've made ciabatta, I have divided the dough into 12 pieces and made oblong rolls. They make the best hot dog buns ever, and are David's favorite thing to make chili dogs with (see recipe below); the ciabatta rolls can absorb a lot of moisture without falling apart. These rolls can also be used for panini or other sandwiches.

Timing

- 8 to 17 hours to prepare the biga
- 3 to 5 minutes to measure ingredients and mix dough
- 3 to 4 hours to ferment dough
- 30 to 60 minutes to shape and proof dough
- 35 to 45 minutes to bake

Equipment you'll definitely need

- Large mixing bowl (stainless steel, glass, Pyrex, or ceramic)
- Wooden spoon
- Large cutting board or clean counter space for shaping dough
- Dough scraper or sharp knife to cut dough

Stuff that's not absolutely necessary but recommended

- Kitchen scale
- 2-quart dough-rising bucket
- KitchenAid or other heavy-duty stand mixer with dough hook
- Baking stone
- Parchment paper

Ingredients	Metric	US	Baker's %
• Prepared biga	167 g	about 1 cup	33
• Unchlorinated water, tepid	425 g	1¾ cups	85
• SAF or other instant yeast	10 g	2 tsp	2
• Unbleached bread flour	500 g	2¼ cups	100
• Sea salt	10 g	1½ tsp	2

Preparing the Biga

Using the master recipe above, start the biga at least 8 hours, and up to 17 hours, before you want to bake your ciabatta. If you are starting your biga from scratch, leave it out at room temperature for 1 hour, then refrigerate it at least 8 more hours. It will double in volume and will smell slightly acidic and look shiny and bubbly. Leave it in the fridge until you're ready to mix your dough. If you made the biga ahead of time, and it's been refrigerated for at least a day, simply follow the directions below.

Mixing the Dough

Take the biga out of the fridge and scrape about 167 g (1 cup) into a large mixing bowl. Pour the water over the biga and stir, breaking the biga up into pieces. Stir in the yeast, flour, and salt until a dough forms.

Kneading the Dough

If kneading by hand, I recommend reserving some of the water until after the dough is kneaded, as mentioned above. With hand-kneading, it is much easier to properly exercise the gluten when the dough is not so wet. Knead the dough as you would any other yeasted bread dough, dipping your hands in water as needed to keep the dough from sticking. Knead for a total of 15 minutes, with a 10-minute rest after each 5 minutes of kneading. Let the dough rest 15 minutes once you're finished kneading, then work in the remaining water with your hands. It may seem like the dough won't absorb the extra water, but it will. Just keep at it, and it will all come together in a few minutes.

If kneading by machine with a dough hook, mix the dough at medium-high speed (8 on a KitchenAid mixer) for about 15 minutes. Be sure to keep an eye on the mixer, because at this speed it can travel around your counter. This dough is very wet, so don't expect it to pull away from the sides of the mixing bowl; every few minutes, scrape it off the sides using a rubber spatula. Now turn up the speed to high (10 on a KitchenAid), and knead another 3 or 4 minutes; at this point, the dough should start to clear the sides of the bowl and form a more solid dough, shiny and very elastic.

Fermenting the Dough

Transfer the dough to your 2-quart dough-rising bucket and put the lid on. Let it ferment at room temperature until the dough triples in volume, filling up the container; this will take 3 to 4 hours. The dough will look airy and very bubbly and active.

Shaping and Proofing the Ciabatta

Put your baking stone on a rack in the middle of the oven and preheat to 475°F (246°C). Be sure the baking stone preheats for at least 45 minutes.

Have ready two pieces of parchment paper, big enough to cover your pizza peel or a rimless cookie sheet. You'll be shaping this dough quickly, with a minimum of handling, so it helps to have the parchment ready first.

Tip the dough out onto a well-floured board or countertop; it will almost pour out, so be prepared to move quickly to keep it from sliding off the edge of the board or counter. Dust the top of the dough with flour, and quickly flip the dough over. If making loaves, divide the dough into two pieces.

Dust the pieces with a little more flour. Pick up one piece at a time, holding one end of the piece in each hand. Lift each piece quickly, stretching it at the same time, and transfer it to the parchment paper. Use your fingertips to dimple the dough, stretching it a little more into the shape and size you want. Don't try to make it look perfect; rough rectangles are fine for buns or rolls. It's best not to over-handle this dough.

When you're finished shaping the dough, dust the tops of the loaves or rolls again with flour, cover loosely with plastic wrap, and let ferment again at room temperature for 30 to 45 minutes.

Baking the Bread

Uncover the loaves or rolls on one piece of parchment paper. Slide it onto your peel and into the oven. Pull on the parchment paper to straighten it out; this dough is very soft. Bake the loaves for 25 to 30 minutes. The crust will be golden brown, and the bread will look puffy. Transfer to a wire cooling rack, still on the parchment paper, and cool for at least 1 hour. This bread is best eaten within a couple of days, which is never a problem at our house.

Variation: Ciabatta Rolls

Ciabatta rolls are easy and so delicious! Just divide the dough into about 12 pieces for hot dog buns or 16 pieces if you want smaller dinner rolls. Dust the pieces with flour, and shape them quickly; I find it's easiest to use my fingertips to gently push the dough pieces into shape right on the parchment they will bake on. Dust the top of the rolls with a little more flour, cover loosely with plastic wrap. Follow the instructions above for proofing and baking ciabatta, except bake rolls for about 20 minutes.

FIGURE 12.3. Ciabatta rolls.

Canyon Creek Farms Chili Dog

- Ciabatta, made into rectangular rolls about 2″ to 3″ wide and 6″ long
- Homemade or good-quality commercial all-beef hot dogs, or bratwurst if preferred
- Fresh chili with beans, preferably homemade, heated but not boiling
- Medium or sharp cheddar cheese, grated
- Sweet onion, finely chopped and lightly sautéed

FIGURE 12.4. Canyon Creek Farms chili dog.

Cook the hot dogs or bratwurst. I like to bring them to a boil briefly in a saucepan, then drain and finish cooking them on the grill. Split a ciabatta roll lengthwise, and spread it open so it lies fairly flat. Depending on the size of your hot dogs, you can split them lengthwise too or leave them as is.

Put the sausage in the middle of the roll. Ladle a generous helping of chili on top. Add a handful of grated cheese, then onion. Don't skimp on toppings.

Sally Lunn

You'll have to excuse my embarking on another self-indulgent nostalgia trip. I never knew the origin of this interesting bread until I looked it up today on Wikipedia; I just knew it was a kind of bread Mum made while we were growing up. It's basically one big sponge, beaten with a whisk or in a mixer, and left to ferment before baking it in a tube pan.

What's up with that name? There are various theories. Wikipedia says it is the original "Bath bun," dating from about 1780. Agatha Christie fans will have heard of Bath buns; I'm also a fan of Anne Perry's Victorian-era detective stories, so I've read about Bath buns but had no idea what they actually were. They originated in the English spa town of Bath and, enriched with cream and eggs, were similar to the French brioche. Charles Dickens's 1845 book *The Chimes* mentions Sally Lunn, along with tea and crumpets. The same year, Eliza Acton's book *Modern Cookery for Private Families* described the Bath bun as "Solimemne, a rich French breakfast cake, or Sally Lunn."

I'm also a fan of Gilbert and Sullivan (yes, my British roots are showing), so I was tickled to find that Sally Lunn is even mentioned in their comic opera *The Sorcerer*:

> *The rollicking bun, and the gay Sally Lunn!*
> *The rollicking, rollicking bun!*

Anyway, let's make Sally Lunn. You can always listen to a Gilbert and Sullivan soundtrack while you're making it. There's nothing quite like a G and S patter song to make the baking go a little faster.

Timing

- 5–10 minutes to measure ingredients and mix dough
- 1 hour to ferment dough
- 45 minutes to proof dough
- 45–50 minutes to bake

Equipment you'll definitely need

- Large mixing bowl (stainless steel, glass, Pyrex, or ceramic)
- Wire whisk and wooden spoon
- 10″ tube pan, lightly greased

Stuff that's not absolutely necessary but recommended

- Kitchen scale
- KitchenAid or other heavy-duty stand mixer with dough hook

Ingredients	Metric	US	Baker's %
• Unchlorinated water, warm (110° to 115°F/43° to 46°C)	118 g	½ cup	17
• SAF or other instant yeast	about 13 g	4½ tsp	1.8
• Milk or heavy cream, lukewarm	345 g	1½ cups	49
• Sea salt	10 g	1½ tsp	1.4
• Eggs, large, beaten	92 g	2	13
• Unsalted butter, softened	57 g	¼ cup	8
• Unbleached all-purpose flour	700 g	about 5¼ cups	100

Mixing the Dough

Put the warm water in a large mixing bowl or the bowl of your stand mixer. Stir in the instant yeast. Add the milk or cream, sugar, sea salt, eggs, butter, and flour. Beat until smooth. Cover the mixing bowl, and let the dough ferment until at least doubled in volume and light and airy-looking, about 1 hour.

Proofing the Dough

Gently deflate the dough with a floured hand or wooden spoon, then pour it into the greased tube pan. Cover and let ferment again until the dough rises to within 1 inch of the top of the tube pan, about 45 minutes.

Baking the Bread

Preheat your oven to 350°F (176°C). Bake the Sally Lunn on a middle rack for 45 to 50 minutes; it will be golden brown and crusty.

Variations on a Theme

Are you starting to notice a pattern here? Or more accurately, a method to my madness? So much about making bread is about improvising, really. I mean, it's flour, salt, yeast, and water, for the most part. You can change things up and more or less accidentally create something new and fabulous, like the baker who created ciabatta; he didn't toss out the dough because it was overly hydrated. He decided to see what would happen if he baked it. The Italians also have several kinds of bread that are practically all biga, with just a little extra flour added before fermentation. The Sally Lunn recipe above is pretty much one big sponge.

There are certain "rules" about baking bread: Most professional bakers would agree that the wetter the dough, the better the bread, and the longer the fermentation time, the more flavor the bread will have. But as in most of life, very few rules about baking are hard and fast. As you move from one comfort zone to another, just keep in mind that recipes aren't engraved in stone; if you want to use a biga instead of commercial yeast, do it. If you want to swap out some of the wheat flour for gluten-free grains, do that. It really is up to you.

I'll bet you're getting hungry by now. Let's take a break and make some pizza!

Pizza

IN THE US, we tend to think of the thickness of crust being the main difference between one pizza and another. It's true that the three pizzas covered in this chapter all have different types of crust. New York-style pizza, Chicago deep-dish pizza, all those big national chains—many of us have grown up thinking that pizza always has a lot of cheese, and the more toppings, the better.

You might be surprised to learn that in Italy, arguably ground zero for pizza lovers, traditional pizza is very different.

There, pizza is all about the bread. Although most kinds of pizza are made with white flour, the way the dough is leavened and fermented results in exceptional flavor and texture in the pizza. Toppings, compared with the American standard, are very light and don't always include cheese. Actually toppings traditionally were whatever leftover bits of meats, vegetables, and fresh herbs were on hand.

I encourage you to get into that mindset with your pizza baking: If you have a herb garden, or you grow your own vegetables, take advantage of what is in season, fresh and delicious. Vary the sauce, or use no sauce at all other than olive oil; use cheese, or not. Who cares if the pizza is different every time? Concentrate on the dough; it's what *makes* pizza.

The following recipes use either commercial yeast or a biga, both techniques you have already learned. Later, when you're comfortable with storage leavens like sourdough starter, you will find it very easy to improvise sourdough versions of these pizzas.

Neapolitan-style Pizza

Neapolitan-style pizza is enjoying a renaissance of sorts in the US. In our area, a number of restaurants have popped up in the past few years, often with wood-fired ovens and dedicated to Neapolitan-style pizza.

Traditional Neapolitan-style pizza is round, about the size of a dinner plate, with a fairly thick rim of crust surrounding a very thin crust.

SEXY SCIENCE TALK

The Mysterious "00" Flour

Some recipes, such as pizza dough and fresh pasta, call for 00 flour (that's double-zero, not oh-oh). It is the most highly refined soft type of wheat flour, almost talcum powder soft. A common misconception is that this softness also means that the flour is low in protein, akin to our cake flour or pastry flour. Actually, the protein content of 00 flour depends on what kind of wheat it's ground from, and it can vary quite a bit. Most 00 flour that we see in the United States is ground from durum wheat and has a mid-range protein content of about 11% to 12%, similar to all-purpose white flour.

I don't usually recommend specific brands of flour, but Antimo Caputo 00 flour is an exception. Caputo 00 flour is ideal for pizza dough for two reasons: it's finely ground, and it has a lower gluten content than most flours. The "00" refers to the texture of the flour: Italian flours are classified by numbers according to how finely they are ground, from the roughest ground "tipo" 1, to 0, and the finest 00. Meanwhile, the Caputo 00 is made from a selection of the finest grains the Caputo family can find to give your dough just enough, but not too much, stretch at 12.5% gluten.

FIGURE 13.1. Neapolitan-style pizza.

The rim makes it easier to hold a slice of pizza as well as keeping the toppings in place during baking. It is ideally baked in a very hot wood-fired oven, at temperatures approaching 900°F (482°C), and the rim will show the classic bit of charring. It bakes very quickly at this temperature; I have baked these pizzas in my wood-fired oven in as little as 90 seconds.

However, you can get very good results baking Neapolitan pizza in your kitchen oven. I definitely recommend using a baking stone, thoroughly preheated, for this or any other pizza baked in your kitchen oven.

Timing

- 3 to 5 minutes to measure ingredients and mix dough
- 8 to 10 minutes to knead
- 1 hour to ferment dough
- 20 to 30 minutes to shape dough and add toppings
- 30 minutes to proof pizzas
- 15 to 30 minutes to bake, depending on size of pizza

Equipment you'll definitely need

- Large mixing bowl (stainless steel, glass, Pyrex, or ceramic)
- Wooden spoon
- Pizza peel or rimless cookie sheet
- Large cutting board or clean counter area for shaping pizza
- Dough scraper or sharp knife

Stuff that's not absolutely necessary but recommended

- Kitchen scale
- 2-quart dough-rising bucket
- Baking stone
- Parchment paper
- Pastry brush

Ingredients	Metric	US	Baker's %
• Unchlorinated water, warm	350 g	1½ cups	70
• SAF or other instant yeast	5 g	1¾ tsp	1
• Extra-virgin olive oil	55 g	¼ cup	11
• Unbleached 00 or all-purpose flour	500 g	3¾ cups	100
• Sea salt	10 g	1½ tsp	2
• Extra olive oil for brushing			

Mixing and Kneading the Dough

Dissolve the yeast in the warm water. Stir in the 55 g (¼ cup) olive oil. Add the salt, then gradually stir in the flour, mixing thoroughly to get all the lumps out. Let the dough rest for about 15 to 20 minutes before kneading.

Knead dough by hand, dipping your hands in water when dough starts to stick, for about 8 minutes. The dough should be fairly firm, but soft.

Fermenting the Dough

Put the dough in a 2-quart dough-rising bucket and put the lid on. Or leave in the mixing bowl and cover with plastic wrap. Let ferment at room temperature until just about doubled in volume; in the dough-rising bucket, the dough will nearly fill the container. If it has not increased this much in volume in an hour, just give it a little more time.

Shaping and Proofing the Pizza

Start preheating your oven and baking stone 1 hour before you plan to bake. Heat the oven to 500°F (260°C). By the time you have shaped your pizza, added toppings, and let it proof, the oven will be ready to bake.

You can either use all the dough to make one large pizza, or divide it into 2 or 3 pieces to make smaller pizzas. If you are new to shaping pizza by hand, I recommend dividing the dough and making smaller pizzas at first; this way you can get comfortable with the process with less pressure. A little prac-

FIGURE 13.2. Neapolitan pizza ready to bake.

tice goes a long way when it comes to shaping pizza!

Pizza can be shaped with a rolling pin, so do this if it is easier for you. For Neapolitan-style pizza, though, I hope you'll try shaping it by hand; I think it's a lot easier to form the classic rounded rim. I like to take a piece of dough, flatten it into a smallish round, then drape it over my fist. Using both fists under the dough, start stretching the dough toward the edges by moving your fists apart and rotating the dough. Don't grasp the edges; you want to stretch the inside of the piece of dough toward the edges, not stretch the edges themselves (Figure 13.2).

You're aiming for a pizza that is ⅛" to ¼" thick at the center, with a rounded rim about ¾" to 1" thick. When it is almost the desired size and shape, lay the pizza on a pizza peel covered with parchment paper. You can sprinkle the paper with cornmeal if you want, but, at least as you're learning, I definitely recommend using the parchment paper; you don't want to know how many times I've screwed up a pizza when some of the dough stuck to the peel just as I was flicking it off the peel and onto the baking stone.

Note: If you're making more than one pizza, I suggest you shape the first one and put it on the peel as described above. Then shape the rest of the pizzas, placing them on sheets of parchment paper on the counter or a handy table.

Let the pizza rest, covered lightly with plastic wrap, for about 30 minutes, or more depending on the temperature in your kitchen. The dough will have risen a little more and should look soft and puffy.

Either use a classic topping like the ones below, or just improvise with whatever bits of fresh tomatoes, cheese, fresh herbs, mushrooms, etc. that you have on hand. Always brush the dough with a little olive oil before adding other toppings.

Toppings for Neapolitan-style Pizza

My good friend Michelle Oss-Payne is a fabulous foodie and my guru of Neapolitan-style pizza. Here is her favorite topping combination, from Fondi in Gig Harbor, WA.

Run a large (28 oz) can of San Marzano-style tomatoes through a coarse food mill, and add 1 teaspoon salt and 1 tablespoon extra-virgin olive oil. Spread a thin layer of the sauce on the prepared crust (see shaping instructions above), then add a few thin slices of fresh mozzarella cheese (don't overdo the cheese) and bake. When the pizza is done, add a few paper-thin slices of prosciutto and fresh arugula leaves, then drizzle the pizza with a balsamic vinegar reduction.

Other traditional toppings include

* The **Margherita** pizza, which is topped with olive oil, thinly sliced tomatoes, fresh mozzarella cheese, fresh basil leaves, and a sprinkle of sea salt
* **Aglio e Olio**: Drizzle the pizza with olive oil, and sprinkle with a few thinly sliced garlic cloves, sea salt, freshly ground pepper, and chopped fresh oregano leaves.

There is a lot of room for creativity and experimenting with pizza toppings; I would just encourage you to embrace the less-is-more philosophy. You put some effort and time into making this wonderful pizza dough, so don't drown out its flavor by slathering on the toppings.

Roman-style Pizza

I first learned about Roman-style pizza in Dan Leader's wonderful book *Local Breads* (see Appendix B). I've never been to Italy, but I have been able to recreate a smaller version of this amazing bread in both my kitchen oven and the wood-fired oven.

This famous pizza, called Pizza Bianca (White Pizza), is simply topped with extra-virgin olive oil and a sprinkle of sea salt. It is stretched very thin, baked quickly in a wood-fired oven, then more olive oil is brushed on just before serving.

The traditional Roman-style pizza, although made with commercial yeast, is challenging to make because of its high water content. This high hydration level, along with high baking heat, results in a very light, bubbly crust but also makes kneading difficult. I recommend kneading it using a heavy mixer like a KitchenAid, with a dough hook, especially if you're not used to working with very wet doughs. If you don't have such a mixer, follow the directions below for hand-kneading.

Timing

- 3 to 5 minutes to measure ingredients and mix dough
- 17 to 20 minutes to knead (see notes below)
- 3 to 4 hours to ferment dough
- 15 to 20 minutes to shape dough and add toppings
- 15 to 20 minutes to bake

Equipment you'll definitely need

- Large mixing bowl (stainless steel, glass, Pyrex, or ceramic)
- Wooden spoon
- Pizza peel or rimless cookie sheet
- Large cutting board or clean counter area for shaping pizza
- Dough scraper or sharp knife

Stuff that's not absolutely necessary but recommended

- Kitchen scale
- 3- or 4-quart dough-rising bucket
- KitchenAid or other heavy-duty stand mixer with dough hook
- Baking stone
- Parchment paper
- Pastry brush

Ingredients	Metric	US	Baker's %
• Unchlorinated water, tepid	435 g	1¾ cups	85
• SAF or other instant yeast	5 g	1 tsp	1
• Unbleached bread flour	500 g	3⅔ cups	100
• Sea salt	10 g	1½ tsp	2
• Olive oil and extra sea salt for topping			

Mixing the Dough

Pour the tepid water into a large mixing bowl or the mixing bowl of your mixer, if using. **Note:** If you're planning to knead this dough by hand, add only 325 grams of the water at this point; the rest will be added when kneading is done.

Add the yeast, flour, and salt, stirring just until all ingredients are blended.

Kneading the Dough

If kneading by hand, I recommend reserving some of the water until after the dough is kneaded, as mentioned above. With hand-kneading, it is much easier to properly exercise the gluten when the dough is not so wet. Knead the dough as you would any other yeasted bread dough, dipping your hands in water as needed to keep the dough from sticking. Knead for a total of 15 minutes, with a 10-minute rest after each 5 minutes of kneading. Let the dough rest 15 minutes once you're finished kneading, then work in the remaining water with your hands. It may seem like the dough won't absorb the extra water, but it will. Just keep at it, and it will all come together in a few minutes.

If kneading by machine with a dough hook, mix the dough at medium-high speed (8 on a KitchenAid mixer) for about 15 minutes. Be sure to keep an eye on the mixer, because at this speed it can travel around your counter. This dough is very wet, so don't expect it to pull away from the sides of the mixing bowl; every few minutes, scrape it off the sides using a rubber spatula. Now turn up the speed to high (10 on a KitchenAid), and knead another 3 or 4 minutes; the dough should now start to clear the sides of the bowl and form a more solid dough, shiny and very elastic.

Fermenting the Dough

Usually I use my 2-quart dough-rising bucket to ferment this amount of bread dough, but in this case the dough will triple in size so you'll need a larger container for fermenting. I often use my 6-quart dough-rising bucket, as I only have 2- and 6-quart sizes. You can ferment the dough in the mixing bowl, covered with plastic, provided it has room to triple in volume. Let it ferment at room temperature (70° to 75°F/21° to 24°C) until tripled in volume, about 3 to 4 hours.

Shaping the Pizza and Adding Toppings

Put your baking stone on a rack in the middle of your oven, and pre-heat oven to 500°F (260°C).

Generously dust the cutting board or counter with flour. Tip the dough out onto the floured surface, scraping the bowl out with a spatula; the dough will be very soft. Divide the dough into 2 equal pieces with the dough scraper or knife. Dust the top of each piece with flour, cover with plastic wrap, and let rest for about 10 minutes.

Cover the pizza peel or a rimless cookie sheet with parchment paper, and dust the paper with flour. With floured hands, transfer one piece of dough to the center of the peel. Use your fingertips to dimple the dough all over, pressing it out into a rectangle. Pick up the dough and turn it, stretching it in the process, and dimple it again. Ideally the rectangle will end up just a little smaller than your baking stone. Don't worry if it doesn't stretch this much, though; it's better not to over-handle the dough. You'll get the hang of it with a little practice, and I promise it's worth the effort.

Use a pastry brush to lightly coat the pizza with olive oil; I usually just drizzle on some olive oil and spread it around lightly with my fingertips. Sprinkle the pizza with sea salt.

Baking the Pizza

Slide the pizza, parchment paper and all, onto the baking stone. Bake for 15 to 20 minutes. The pizza will be bubbly and golden brown; if it's a little charred around the edges (as it is when I bake pizza in my wood-fired oven), this is a good thing.

I usually shape and top the second pizza while the first is baking. Just put a piece of parchment paper on the counter, shape the pizza, and it will be ready to go once the first pizza is out of the oven.

Sicilian-style Pizza

According to Carol Field's lovely book *The Italian Baker* (see Appendix B), the topping for Sicilian pizza traditionally includes the well-known ingredients of the country: anchovies, tomatoes, and local cheese and herbs. Sicilian pizza crust is a little thicker than Roman or Neapolitan pizza, and the pizza is baked at a slightly lower temperature. I hope you'll try all three pizza types in this chapter and decide for yourself which is your favorite. Again, play with the toppings!

Timing

- 3–5 minutes to measure ingredients and mix dough
- 10–12 minutes to knead dough
- 1½ hours to ferment dough
- 20–30 minutes to shape dough and prepare toppings
- 30–35 minutes to bake

Equipment you'll definitely need

- Large mixing bowl (stainless steel, glass, Pyrex, or ceramic)
- Wooden spoon
- Pizza peel or rimless cookie sheet
- Large cutting board or clean counter area for shaping pizza
- Rolling pin

Stuff that's not absolutely necessary but recommended

- Kitchen scale
- 2-quart dough-rising bucket
- Baking stone
- Parchment paper
- Pastry brush

Ingredients	Metric	US	Baker's %
• Unchlorinated water, warm	350 g	1½ cups	70
• SAF or other instant yeast	7 g	2¼ tsp	1
• Extra-virgin olive oil or lard	30 g	2 Tbsp	6
• Unbleached all-purpose flour	500 g	3¾ cups	100
• Sea salt	10 g	1½ tsp	2

Mixing and Kneading the Dough

Dissolve the yeast in the warm water. Stir in the olive oil or lard. Using a wire whisk, stir in the salt and gradually add about half the flour. Stir in the remaining flour with a wooden spoon, mixing until the dough comes together. Knead the dough for 10 to 12 minutes, dipping your hands in water as needed to keep the dough from sticking.

Fermenting the Dough

In a 2-quart dough-rising bucket with lid, or the mixing bowl covered with plastic wrap, ferment the dough at room temperature until nearly doubled, about 1 hour. In a dough-rising bucket, it will just about fill the bucket when it is ready. Gently deflate the dough with your hand (do not punch it down), cover, and ferment another 20 minutes.

Shaping the Pizza and Adding Toppings

Put your baking stone on a rack in the middle of the oven, and preheat to 425°F (218°C).

Tip the dough onto a floured board or countertop. Flatten it with your hands to a flat disk, then use the rolling pin to roll it out to a circle about 12" in diameter and about ¼" thick. It helps to turn the dough over a few times while rolling it out; also, try rolling it then letting it rest a few minutes before rolling it out to the final size. This helps the dough relax a little and not shrink back on itself so much. Slowing down the pace definitely is an asset here.

Transfer the dough to a pizza peel covered with parchment paper and add toppings as follows.

Topping ingredients	Metric	US
• Large anchovies, rinsed and finely chopped	about 60 g	3
• Mild provolone cheese, grated	25 g	¼ cup
• Artichoke hearts, drained and chopped	120 g	1 cup
• Sfinciuni tomato sauce (recipe below)		
• Extra-virgin olive oil	15 g	1 Tbsp
• Dried oregano	1.5 g	2 tsp
• Prosciutto, coarsely chopped	60 g	½ cup
• Fresh mozzarella cheese, thinly sliced	85 g	½ cup
• Sea salt		
• Freshly ground pepper		
• Extra olive oil for brushing		

Spread the chopped anchovies, half of the provolone cheese, and most of the artichoke hearts over the pizza dough. Drizzle on half the tomato sauce, then half the oregano, and salt and pepper to taste. Drizzle the pizza with olive oil and the rest of the tomato sauce.

Baking the Pizza

Slide the pizza, parchment paper and all, onto the preheated baking stone. Bake for 20 to 25 minutes; the crust will be crispy. Take it out of the oven and add the prosciutto, the rest of the artichoke hearts and oregano, and the fresh mozzarella; then top with the remaining provolone cheese. Bake another 5 to 10 minutes, or until the cheese is completely melted. Remove from oven and brush the edge of the crust with olive oil.

Sfinciuni Tomato Sauce

Bring the water to boil in a large saucepan and simmer the chopped onions, covered, for about 1 hour. Add the remaining ingredients and simmer, covered, for at least another hour. Cool to room temperature before using.

Ingredients	Metric	US
• Large yellow onions, chopped		2
• Water	960 g	4 cups
• Ripe tomatoes, large, peeled, and chopped	900 g	4 or 5 (about 2 pounds)
• Tomato paste	30 g	2 Tbsp
• Olive oil	30 g	2 Tbsp
• Anchovy, drained and chopped		1

PART FOUR

SOURDOUGH AND OTHER BREADS MADE WITH A STORAGE LEAVEN

Levain, Desem, Barm: Introducing Sourdough Starters

What Is a Storage Leaven or Starter?

There are several different names for various types of storage leavens: the French *levain*, Flemish *desem* (or desum), English *barm*, or the more general term *sourdough* or *sourdough starter*. There are slight differences in the way each of these leavens is cultivated, stored, and used, but all serve the same purpose: They leaven and flavor the bread that is made from them. Each is cultivated over a period of days, usually relying on wild yeast rather than commercial yeast, like pre-ferments. Then the leaven is stored in the refrigerator, periodically refreshed or fed, and used to leaven bread.

"Sourdough" Is Not a Flavor

A lot of commercially made bread is labeled "sourdough." There are specific advantages to baking bread with sourdough starter instead of commercial yeast, so it's important to understand the differences. *Saccharomyces cerevisiae* (commercial yeast) has been bred to multiply very quickly during fermentation, which is why dough leavened with it begins rising almost immediately when dough is mixed up. This accelerated fermentation makes it possible for commercial bread to be mass-produced in an amazingly short time. However, it also results in more oxygen in the dough, which ultimately causes the bread to stale more quickly. Short fermentation time also means blander bread.

Wild yeast, of which millions of strains exist, is *S. exiguus*. The whitish bloom one may see on fresh grapes, plums, etc. is also present on grains, in your flour—pretty much everywhere, actually. Wild yeast reproduces at a much slower rate than commercial yeast, so dough rises more slowly. Slowing down the fermentation process this way results in more flavor, though, because it encourages growth of the acid-producing lactobacillus bacteria, which are largely responsible for the flavors associated with sourdough bread. To a point, this acid production is a good thing, because these acids contribute much of the flavor in bread. The acidification that results from long fermentation can break down the gluten in the starter.

Sourdough bread ranks lower on the glycemic index than bread made with commercial yeast. I suspect this is partly because a lot of the various sugars (glucose, fructose, and maltose) in the grain have been consumed by yeast and bacteria during the much longer fermentation process. If your doctor says you can eat sourdough bread (for example, if you are diabetic), be sure to read the labels on bread you buy. These days, what I have been seeing most often on sourdough bread labels is "sour culture." Mass-produced bread labeled "sourdough" is often made with commercial yeast and has had a souring agent added (like citric acid). This is sourdough-*flavored* bread, not what your doctor means!

So what makes "sourdough" bread sour, if it's not fermented with sourdough starter? There are some commercially available sourdough "flavors," which vary in content, but most have at least some citric acid and sometimes a blend of acids including tartaric acid or malic acid. If you make your own wine, you probably have one or more of these acids among your wine-making ingredients. Having never used any of these ingredients to flavor my bread, I can't make any specific recommenda-

SEXY SCIENCE TALK

What's Going on in There?

Sourdough starter, in whatever form, is basically a melting pot that allows for the symbiotic interaction between Candida milleri (a yeast fungus present in sourdough cultures) and lactic bacteria such as L. sanfranciscensis, the bacteria strain that makes San Francisco sourdough bread so famous. You already know that yeast consumes sugars during fermentation, and so do the bacteria. They don't compete for sugars, however; lactobacilli eat maltose, which is not metabolized by C. milleri. Enzymes and lactobacillus release glucose and fructose sugars in the starch that are metabolized by C. milleri and other yeast strains present.

Unlike most yeast, C. milleri can survive in an acidic environment.

tions. One person I spoke to after a presentation said he had tried a sourdough "flavor enhancer" (he didn't know the content or brand) and didn't like the results. I'd say, if you are curious and want to try it, or just don't feel like bothering with sourdough starter just yet, go ahead and try it! Be sure to follow the recommendations of the amount to use, though; I suspect the man who didn't like the flavor of his bread may have added a little extra, hoping for an even more sour bread.

Contrasting Levain, Desem, and Barm

Many people think that levain, desem, and barm are simply different names for the same thing, and in one sense that's true; as mentioned above, they are all wild yeast-based cultures, cultivated and maintained for the purpose of leavening bread dough. So how are they different from each other? Why would you choose one over the others? Here's a brief look at these three storage leavens.

Levain

This, to my mind, is the simplest of these three storage leavens to cultivate and maintain. It can be used for many different types of bread, and that versatility also appeals to me; by varying the kind of flour and amount of water I use to refresh it, I can make sourdough rye, multigrain, or Italian-style white breads, all from one storage leaven.

Levain starters are typically fairly mild. The stiffer consistency promotes slower fermentation and therefore less acid buildup than the thinner, more active barm. The levain I use has only three ingredients: bread flour, whole wheat flour, and water. Kept refrigerated, it need be refreshed only once every week or even two weeks. In Chapter 15, I'll be going into more detail about making your own levain starter and using it to make sourdough bread.

Desem

According to *The Laurel's Kitchen Bread Book* (see Appendix B), it takes about two weeks to get a successful desem (*desem* is Flemish for "starter") going. From then on, it needs to be fed twice a week and, ideally, used to bake bread at least once a week. It takes a lot of fresh whole wheat flour; for the first week or so the desem dough is "incubated" in a big bag (10 pounds or more) of flour before being transferred to a covered container for the rest of the cultivation process. The desem itself is made from about 2 pounds of flour.

As you can see, there is some investment in materials and time to successfully cultivate a desem starter. It can be a challenging process to complete, but enthusiasts say the bread made from desem is better than any other kind. It is an excellent choice of starter if you are going to be making whole-grain breads regularly. I highly recommend *The Laurel's Kitchen Bread Book* if you are interested in learning this method; I think of it as the bible of desem-based bread.

Barm

Barm is the English term for "starter." It is similar to a sponge (see Chapter 12), except it is stored and maintained like levain and desem starters. According to Monica Spiller of The Whole Grain Connection (wholegrainconnection.org), barm starters will be most active when they are refreshed two to four times per week and used to make bread within two days of refreshing. Barm is thinner in consistency than levain or desem, so it ferments faster, especially during warm weather.

As with desem, it can be tricky getting a successful barm up and running. If you want to try it, an easy way to get started is to purchase dried barm; you simply hydrate it with water, and it will be ready to use for bread-baking within about 48 hours. A good source of dried barm is sustainablegrains.org.

Another way to initiate a barm starter is with part organic whole wheat flour and part organic wheat grains, sprouted and ground to a dough-like batter in a food processor. Keeping track of the increased acidity by measuring the barm's pH level is fairly critical to its success, and the process can take two weeks or more, but the results are well worth the effort. Personally I am drawn to this kind of starter simply because it has such a long history with home bread bakers and is largely unknown in the US. Sure, it takes some time and attention, but do try it sometime. There are excellent instructions and detailed methods for making and refreshing barms, as well as making fantastic barm breads, on the Whole Grain Connection website (wholegrainconnection.org).

Where to Start with Your Starter

In the spirit of keeping things as low-maintenance and comfortable as possible, I suggest going with levain if you're just starting out with storage leavens. As with bread in general, there are many ways to tweak your storage leaven: make it thinner or thicker to vary the fermentation time; use all whole-grain flour; or try using sprouted grains, non-gluten grains, or a mix of different grains. Whichever method you eventually land on as your particular comfort zone, you can be sure that your starter, brought to life with the native wild yeasts in your environment and kept alive and thriving with just a little regular attention, will be as unique as the bread you make from it.

Comfort Zone 4: Making Your First Sourdough Starter

15

THERE IS AN ALMOST unbelievable assortment of methods for making your own sourdough starter. I have read through many bread books in the course of research, some from the 1970s, some published just a year or two ago. If I didn't already have a starter going, I might very well have been too intimidated to try after reading some of those methods. Some were thicker, some thinner in consistency; some were all white flour, some several types of flour; an amazing number of recipes called for sugar, honey, or other sweeteners. Some methods required several feedings every day, and were very strict about the temperature needs of the apparently mysterious and temperamental mixture.

Let me simplify it for you. To make a sourdough starter (storage levain), you'll need flour and water. That's all. The wild yeasts and lactobacillus bacteria that populate a healthy sourdough starter are on the grain, they're in the air, they're on that bunch of grapes in your fruit bowl. You don't need to add sugar or honey to "feed" the yeast; it will find plenty of carbohydrates in the grain to keep it happy. And please don't add salt; it inhibits fermentation, which would kind of defeat the purpose of cultivating a starter.

The amount of time it takes to get a starter going varies depending on room temperature, type of flour used, and the consistency of the culture. Generally speaking, you can expect your starter to be active and ready to use within 3 to 7 days. My storage levain has been going since late 2009, and I've given away lots of it as gifts or at demonstrations. It's flour and water, you know, providing a homey environment for microscopic yeasts and bacteria; sometimes it seems like there's an element of magic or alchemy involved, but it's easy. Here we go.

Starting Your Starter
(Low-maintenance Levain)

Tips

- Use spring water if possible; bottled is fine. Avoid chlorinated water and distilled water.
- Use organic, stone-ground flour for activating your starter.
- Rye flour is added on the first day, as it ferments quickly and has more enzymes and minerals than wheat flour, helping to get a new culture off to a strong start.

FIGURE 15.1. Starter ingredients just after mixing: Day 1.

- I recommend putting a lid on your starter container. The yeast and bacteria are already in there; there's no need to use cheesecloth or anything else as a revolving door. Trust me on this.
- The ingredient measurements are not critical. It's easier, when doing this for the first time, to have the parameters defined, but don't worry about it being exact. The main thing to keep in mind is to keep all the flour in the mix well hydrated.

Equipment you will need

- Medium-sized mixing bowl
- 1-quart clear container, with a lid. I like the dough-rising buckets from King Arthur Flour, which come in several sizes. A wide-mouth Mason jar will work too, although I find a wider, shorter container makes it easier to add and mix ingredients.

Day 1

- Pour into a bowl: 75 g (⅓ cup) spring water, tepid
- Stir in 50 g (⅓ cup) organic unbleached stone-ground bread or all-purpose flour and 50 g (⅓ cup) organic stone-ground fine rye flour. Stir till all the flour has been moistened. Dough will be tacky.
- Cover the bowl with plastic wrap and let it stand at room temperature for 24 hours.

Day 2

- The culture will look much the same as on Day 1, although it may have risen slightly.
- Add 30 g (2 tablespoons) tepid spring water, 50 g (⅓ cup) organic unbleached stone-ground bread or all-purpose flour, and 5 g (1 tablespoon) organic stone-ground whole wheat flour.
- Stir to blend. If needed, knead briefly to incorporate all the flour.
- Cover the bowl with plastic wrap, and let stand at room temperature for 24 hours.

FIGURE 15.2. Day 3 of starter development.

Day 3

- Your culture will have expanded 1½ to 2 times its original volume. You should see bubbles forming below the surface, and the smell will be slightly yeasty and fruity.
- Repeat feeding steps of Day 2; cover and let stand at room temperature for 24 hours.

Day 4 and on

- Your levain may be ready to use any time in the next few days. When it's ready, you will observe most or all of the following:
  - Surface of culture looks dimpled or bubbly and may rise to a dome.
  - Smells like ripe, slightly sour fruit and tastes tangy, like citrus fruit.
  - Cutting through with a paring knife shows air pockets trapped by gluten strands.
  - If it doesn't already look like this, simply repeat Day 3 steps until it does.
- Transfer levain to 1-quart container and put on lid.
- Store levain in refrigerator and refresh once a week by following Day 2 steps.

FIGURE 15.3. Fully developed starter, Day 5: Volume has more than doubled, and starter is bubbly and stretchy.

Refreshing Your Starter Before Making Bread

I usually bake sourdough bread once a week. I like to keep my starter fairly stiff; this slows down the fermentation so I don't have to refresh it more frequently. Having done this for a number of years, I'm used to the routine and never really measure the flour and water for refreshing the starter. Rather, I pay more attention to the consistency, aiming for a mix in which the flour is all thoroughly moistened but just barely. Remember, the thinner the mixture, the faster it ferments. (This is true of dough as well as starter, by the way.) If you're planning to bake bread more often than weekly, make the starter a little thinner when you refresh it; otherwise, keeping it fairly stiff enables you to wait longer before refreshing and using it, without worrying about excess acid buildup.

TIP

Once your starter is cultivated, active, and bubbly, please keep it in the fridge! At room temperatures or warmer, the starter will ferment much more quickly, requiring frequent refreshment in order to avoid excessive acid buildup. The cool temperature in your refrigerator won't kill those yeasts, I promise; they simply work at a more leisurely pace. When you take the starter out to refresh or use it, you will see that it has increased in volume.

I generally use only a small amount of flour and water to refresh my starter, since I keep a fairly small amount of it going in the fridge. My rule of thumb: By weight, I use about twice as much flour as water; a typical refreshment would be about 50 g water and 100 g flour. This will vary a bit depending on what kind of flour you use, since some flours absorb more water than others. So again, I find it easier to pay attention to the consistency; if it seems too dry, add a little water. If it seems too wet, add a little flour.

One thing that seems to lead to a lot of confusion is how much starter you need to make your bread. Some folks I've spoken to keep their starter going for weeks without using it, then they use all of it at once to make bread and start all over with a new culture. As I said, there is so much conflicting and sometimes confusing information out there. It's actually not complicated or mysterious, and although it might seem a little fussy at first, you'll soon get used to the routine.

Method: Refreshing Levain Prior to Baking (for one loaf of bread)

Ingredients	Metric	US	Baker's %
• Levain starter	45 g	¼ cup	45
• Unchlorinated water, tepid	50 g	scant ¼ cup	50
• Unbleached all-purpose or Type 55 flour	95 g	⅔ cup	95
• Stone-ground whole wheat flour	5 g	2 tsp	5

Storage Levain and Bread Levain

Okay, so here's what you do. About 12 hours before you plan to mix the dough (and about 24 hours before you plan to bake the bread), you want to get some starter going; I'll call this your bread levain. Take your container of storage levain from the fridge; scoop out a small amount, and put it into a small mixing bowl. How much you use isn't critical, but try to use at least 45 g (¼ cup) for each loaf you plan to bake. Some sources advise using more in cold weather and less in warm weather. I never remember to do that, and I am so used to the long fermentation times in my cool kitchen, if it takes another hour or so when it's cold, it really doesn't matter.

Now add flour and water to both starters, using the ingredient list above as a guideline. Once you've refreshed both starters, cover them and let them ferment at room temperature. Leave the bread levain out until you are ready to mix up your dough; let the storage levain stay out for at least an hour, then put it back into the fridge.

FIGURE 15.4. Refreshing starter prior to mixing bread dough.

FIGURE 15.5. The storage levain (*left*) goes back in the fridge; the bread levain (*right*) will be used to make bread.

SEXY SCIENCE TALK

How Much Starter (Storage Levain) Do I Need to Keep It Going?

One gram (⅟₂₈ ounce) of sourdough starter has around 1 billion lactobacilli and 10 million yeast cells; as long as it is refreshed regularly so the little critters have a steady food supply, your culture will be active and healthy. So you can see that maintaining a large amount of starter isn't necessary. I usually keep about 1½ cups or so as my storage leaven. Sometimes I will increase that temporarily, if I have a presentation or demonstration coming up, but otherwise I just keep that small amount going.

TIP

It's a myth that the older the starter, the better it is. It's true that over time your starter will become more heavily populated with local yeast and bacteria, but regular refreshing is necessary to avoid the breakdown of gluten caused by overly acid conditions. Don't make the mistake of letting it go on and on without refreshment, in the hope that the flavor will get more sour. There is definitely a point of diminishing returns on that; the yeast can survive only a certain amount of acidity; ditto the gluten. The flavor of the finished bread has a lot more to do with the length of time the dough has fermented before baking than with how sour or acidic the starter has become.

What About Discarding Some of the Starter?

Oh, boy. I have seen so many starter methods that advocate this thing of adding a lot of flour and water every day till you have a fairly huge amount of starter. Then you're told to throw out half of it or more! I think this is a needless waste, and I can't imagine anyone enjoys doing it, not after they've spent several days and good ingredients getting to that point.

Of course, it's easier to store a smaller amount of starter than a large amount. If you have more than you need, or find you're just not using it very often so it builds up every time you refresh it, there are a few steps you can take. First, use some of the excess to bake something! Even plain white-flour biscuits and pancakes benefit from the slight acidity and nice yeast action in that

---

SEXY SCIENCE TALK

What Makes Sourdough Sour? Production of Lactic and Acetic Acids During Fermentation

Why are lactic and acetic acids important? Lactic acid affects taste, especially in long-fermented breads like sourdough; acetic acid affects aroma.

Production of lactic acid in dough is determined mainly by the ash content (buffering capacity) of the flour. Lactic acid production increases when fermentation time speeds up at warmer temperatures.

The amount of acetic acid produced during fermentation is controlled mainly by the availability of fructose. There is a lot of fructose in dough, but not all of it is available to the acid-producing lactobacilli.

Adding 1% to 2% sucrose (table sugar, a combination of glucose and fructose) by weight to the dough increases acetic acid content. It's important to note that, while yeasts tolerate low pH, yeast activity is inhibited by acetic acid. Given adequate fermentation time, yeast gets plenty of food from the starches in the flour, so for most kinds of bread, adding sugar is not necessary and not recommended.

Acidity in sourdough culture and dough weakens the gluten network by increasing the number of positively charged amino acids along the protein chains and increasing the repulsive forces between chains. In sourdough bread, salt helps limit the protein-digesting activity of the souring bacteria, which can otherwise damage the gluten.

---

starter. Just put the extra in a separate container, marked "Use first," and have fun looking up and trying recipes.

Second, give it away. You have no idea how thrilled your friends and neighbors will be to receive a gift of fresh, lively sourdough starter. You already know there's no big mystery to making a starter, but chances are they don't, and I promise it will be much appreciated, especially if you give them a copy of this book to go with it!

Third, freeze your starter. If you're not using it very often, rather than continuing to feed it weekly (which eventually will start making you feel guilty), freeze it. I would definitely put it in the freezer shortly after refreshing it so the acidity level is relatively low. Freezing doesn't kill the yeast; it simply goes dormant. When you do get back to baking, just thaw it in the fridge for a day or two to let it come back to life gradually. Once it's thawed, add a little flour and water (it will be hungry after its long nap), let it ferment all day or all night, then you're good to go.

What About Using Grapes or Raisins to Get a Starter Going?

If you've ever noticed a whitish "bloom" on the skins of grapes or raisins, guess what—that's wild yeast. I've never actually cultivated a starter from scratch using grapes or raisins, but I have used raisins to jump-start a sluggish fermentation—once, for example, years ago, when I was trying to get a starter going using flour that was, as Agatha Christie would say, not in its first youth.

I think it's easier to use raisins for this. All you need to do is put the raisins in a bowl and pour in enough warm water to cover them. Not *hot* water; it doesn't take a lot of excess heat to kill off the yeast. Let the raisins soak for about 15 to 20 minutes, then drain off the water and add it to your starter or dough.

I would definitely use organic raisins or grapes for this to avoid sulfur or pesticide residues that might be present on the non-organic type. Remember, these are wild yeasts, native to wherever the grapes were grown, so unless you grow your own, you might notice a slight variation in the flavor of the dough or starter as it ferments.

Isn't this fun? I could happily spend a lot of my spare time just experimenting with sourdough starter. Results can vary a lot, depending on what kind of flour you use and the consistency of the starter. When you're ready, flip to the next chapter, and I'll walk you through the process of using that starter to make your first loaf of sourdough bread. If you've come this far, when you never thought this would ever be your comfort zone, pat yourself on the back; that is a real accomplishment, and I'm so happy for you!

Making Long-fermented Sourdough Bread

16

Good bread is the most fundamentally satisfying of all foods;
and good bread with fresh butter, the greatest of feasts.
— JAMES BEARD

 I MOST OFTEN MAKE free-form loaf bread, like this classic French-style mild sourdough. This simple recipe using unbleached bread flour, plus some whole wheat and rye flour, assumes you have refreshed your sourdough starter 8 to 12 hours before you mix your dough, following the instructions in Chapter 15.

Like most recipes in this book, it uses a total of 500 grams of flour and makes a good-sized loaf. This dough has a moderate hydration rate and is easy to shape into round or oblong loaves. Its relatively high percentage of bread flour consistently results in a bread that rises strongly during both fermentation and baking.

Long-fermented Sourdough Bread

Timing

- 8 to 12 hours to refresh sourdough
- 30 to 60 minutes to mix and knead dough

- 8 to 12 hours to ferment dough
- 1 hour to shape and proof dough
- 50 minutes to bake

Equipment you'll definitely need

- Large mixing bowl (stainless steel, glass, Pyrex, or ceramic)
- Wooden spoon
- Large cutting board for shaping
- Parchment paper
- Sharp serrated bread knife or lame for slashing the loaf

Stuff that's not absolutely necessary but recommended

- Kitchen scale
- 2-quart dough-rising bucket with lid
- Banneton or other proofing basket
- Baking stone
- Pizza peel or rimless cookie sheet

Ingredients	Metric	US	Baker's %
• Levain, refreshed	195 g	about 1 cup	40
• Unchlorinated water, cool	350 g	1½ cups	70
• Unbleached bread flour	375 g	2¾ cups	75
• Stone-ground whole wheat flour	100 g	¾ cup	20
• Rye flour	25 g	3 Tbsp	5
• Sea salt	10 g	1½ tsp	2

Mixing the Dough

Put the water and three flours into a large mixing bowl. Stir to blend, making sure all of the flour is moistened. Let the dough rest for 15 to 20 minutes.

Kneading the Dough

Add the levain and salt to the dough. Knead for a total of 10 to 15 minutes. I recommend spacing it out like this: Knead for 5 minutes, let the dough rest for 10 minutes; knead 5, rest 10, and knead 5. Yes, this takes longer overall, but you will find that after the first 10-minute rest, the dough is easier to knead the next time around. That's because the gluten, which you have been working hard while kneading, has had a chance to relax. It really does make the kneading process easier.

I also recommend dipping your kneading hand in cool water as you knead. I keep a small bowl of cool water next to my mixing bowl and dip my hand into it whenever the dough starts to stick to my hand. This makes kneading a little easier, keeps the dough from becoming dry from the addition of flour, and results in a beautifully moist finished loaf.

Fermenting the Dough

If you have a dough-rising bucket, put the dough into it and put on the lid. I know I've repeated this, but I love the 2-quart dough-rising bucket; it makes it so simple to know when a 500-gram batch of dough has finished fermenting—when the bucket is full, it's ready. If you don't have a dough bucket, simply leave the dough in the mixing bowl after kneading and cover it with plastic wrap or a clean, slightly damp kitchen towel. Let it ferment at room temperature until doubled in volume; in my cool kitchen, this consistently takes 10 to 12 hours. I like to mix it up in the evening, let it ferment all night, and it is ready to shape, proof, and bake in the morning.

Shaping, Proofing, and Baking the Bread

When fermentation is finished, preheat your oven and baking stone to 475°F (246°C). After 1 hour, the stone is good and hot. If you are not using a baking stone, preheat the oven for at least 15 minutes.

Shape the dough as desired. If using a banneton (or other proofing bowl or basket), be sure to put the dough into the basket or bowl seam side up, as you will be turning it over onto the parchment paper or baking sheet. Let the dough proof at room temperature for 1 hour while oven preheats.

Put a piece of parchment paper on your pizza peel, if using a baking stone; otherwise, put the parchment on a baking sheet. You can sprinkle some cornmeal or coarse semolina on the parchment if you want. Turn dough quickly onto the parchment paper, and slash the loaf as desired, using the bread knife or lame. Slide the loaf, still on the parchment paper, quickly onto the baking stone (or a middle rack if using a baking sheet). Bake for 45 to 50 minutes.

At this temperature, the edges of dough around the slash marks may be very dark, almost black. This not only is normal, it is a sign of a well-baked loaf.

Cool bread on rack for at least 1 hour before slicing. Once it is cut, store the loaf in a plastic bag.

Variations on Basic Sourdough Bread

No-knead Sourdough Bread

Guess what? There are no hard-and-fast rules about making bread. Stick with recipes if that's your comfort zone; but if you feel adventurous, or simply want to make bread-making a bit more convenient when life gets hectic, you can mix and match techniques, like using the no-knead technique for making sourdough bread.

This is pretty much just what it sounds like. Follow the directions above for making basic sourdough bread, just don't knead the dough. After you have mixed the dough and let it rest, stir in the salt and levain as usual, and stir for about another minute or so. Then continue with the rest of the directions. How easy was that!

The no-knead technique results in fewer and larger air cells in the dough, and thus a more coarse, irregular texture in the finished bread. At the beginning of fermentation, the gluten is less developed than in kneaded dough, but gluten continues to develop during fermentation. So, no-knead doughs definitely benefit from slow fermentation.

This is just one variation on the theme of bread-making. I already know you're creative and imaginative; you bought this book, right? There are probably limitless ways to improvise with these techniques and comfort zones to fit your life, your level of experience, or your sense of adventure.

Whole-grain Sourdough Breads

We've been told for years to eat more whole grains. Recent research shows that breads made with whole grains (especially sourdough breads) have definite benefits for people with sugar sensitivity and diabetes. One such benefit is that the dietary fiber in whole grains considerably slows the breakdown of starch into sugars during the digestive process. The starches in highly processed white flour—for example, fast-food burger buns—start to break down into sugars as soon as you take a bite; your saliva contains the enzyme amylase, which very efficiently converts starch to sugar. With no fiber to speak of left in that flour, that sugar quickly enters the bloodstream, causing a blood-sugar spike.

I think it's ironic that, for many years, grain millers have been supplementing wheat flour with malted wheat or barley. The process of malting activates the very same enzyme, amylase.

So there you go. Another reason to avoid highly processed white flour. And by the way, this caution also applies to many gluten-free flours, which are often just as highly processed as wheat flours.

Working with whole grains in making sourdough bread involves adjusting hydration, because whole-grain flour absorbs more liquid than other flours. The long fermentation typical of the sourdough bread process makes a big difference in the final texture and flavor of whole-grain bread, challenging the stereotype of "health store" bread and whole-wheat bread in general.

See Chapter 4 for discussion on using sprouted grains. If you like to add seeds and nuts to your bread, there are detailed instructions in Chapter 10.

Modifying Your Starter for Specific Kinds of Bread

What if you want to use your mild wheat-flour levain to make, say, a German-style sourdough rye bread? When I was still pretty new to sourdough, I had several different starters that I attempted to keep going at the same time. I had a typical levain, a rye starter, and an interesting starter made from semolina flour. (This one also had a little plain yogurt in it, which adds lactobacillus culture to the starter.) Except for the gluten-free version, I eventually learned to simply keep one storage leaven and modify it when necessary for a particular result.

Here's how it works. When I'm preparing to make bread, I take my storage leaven out of the fridge and scoop out a little bit into a small mixing bowl. This is the one I will refresh and later use when I mix my bread dough. (The rest of the starter goes back in the fridge, once I've added a little flour and water to it.) If I'm going to make whole wheat bread, I use mostly whole wheat flour to refresh my starter; if I'm making sourdough rye, I use more rye flour than white.

This is so much easier! I remember getting fairly stressed trying to keep up with the schedule of refreshing the different starters, especially the rye one, which ferments much more quickly than wheat starter. It took me quite a while to figure this one out, and it makes a lot more sense.

Comfort Zone 5: Sourdough and Yeasted Rye Breads

17

RYE IS OFTEN OVERLOOKED, at least by American home bakers. It's too bad, because rye flour has a wonderful flavor. It's a little tricky to work with, mainly because it has much less gluten than wheat. It is therefore used most often in relatively small quantities along with wheat flour; the gluten in wheat ensures a good rise to the dough during fermentation and baking.

My mother's family has deep roots in Germany, so I suppose it was inevitable that I would discover and fall in love with German sourdough rye breads. The cool climate in much of the country is ideal for growing rye, and the variety of rye-based breads is fascinating. Yes, rye can be a challenge to bake with, but you'll have to trust me that it is worth pushing the boundaries of your comfort zone.

Many people, at least in the US, think caraway seed is what rye bread tastes like. There are even "rye flavors" that home bakers can add to their dough, but these don't have even a hint of the actual flavor of the rye grain. In the US, most commercially baked "rye" bread actually contains very little rye flour. The huge mixing machines of large bakeries aren't really designed to handle the softer, stickier consistency of rye dough. In Germany, though, many breads and crackers are made with a high proportion of rye.

So, given rye's relative lack of gluten, how do those breads rise as well as they do? The secret is the sourdough base. Some rye breads have a little commercial yeast added, but many traditional ryes rely instead on a rye-based sourdough starter. (See Sexy Science Talk below.)

Here is a simple yeasted rye bread that utilizes a sponge preferment, which you're already familiar with. Rye bread, because of the beneficial effect of acidity on the starches, is really at its best when made with a sourdough starter; however, this modified version lets you get your toe in the water without jumping into the deep end of this comfort zone. It's probably easier at first to make this bread in a standard loaf pan.

SEXY SCIENCE TALK

What Are Pentosans and Why Do They Matter?

The pentosans in rye tend to break down the grain's starch during the fermentation process. If the dough is made with commercial yeast, this breakdown of starch would cause the dough to collapse on itself. However, the acidity of the sourdough base greatly limits this, preserving the integrity of the starch granules. This allows the fragile gluten strands to form an elastic network that, while not as strong as wheat's gluten chain, nevertheless is adequate to allow the rye dough to rise and maintain its structure.

Yeasted Rye Bread with Sponge Starter

Timing

- 3 to 5 minutes to measure ingredients and mix sponge
- 4 hours to ferment sponge
- 10 to 25 minutes to mix and knead dough
- 90 minutes to ferment dough
- 60 to 90 minutes to shape and proof dough
- 45 to 55 minutes to bake

Equipment you'll definitely need

- Large mixing bowl (stainless steel, glass, Pyrex, or ceramic)
- Wooden spoon and wire whisk
- Large wooden cutting board
- Standard bread loaf pan

Stuff that's not absolutely necessary but recommended

- Kitchen scale
- 2-quart dough-rising bucket

Sponge ingredients	Metric	US	Baker's %
• Unbleached bread flour	150 g	about 1 cup	50
• Rye flour, preferably stone-ground	150 g	about 1¼ cups	50
• SAF or other instant yeast	4 g	1 tsp	1
• Unchlorinated water, cool	236 g	1 cup	89

Bread ingredients	Metric	US	Baker's %
• Unbleached bread flour	275 g	2 cups	100
• Sea salt	7 g	1¼ tsp	2.5
• SAF or other instant yeast	3 g	1 tsp	11
• Caraway seeds	8 g	1 Tbsp	2.9
• Milk or buttermilk	57 g	¼ cup	22

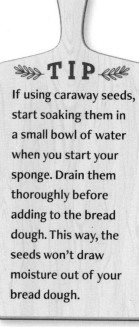

TIP

If using caraway seeds, start soaking them in a small bowl of water when you start your sponge. Drain them thoroughly before adding to the bread dough. This way, the seeds won't draw moisture out of your bread dough.

Making the Sponge

In a large mixing bowl, stir all the sponge ingredients together with a wooden spoon or wire whisk to make a smooth batter. Cover the bowl with plastic wrap and ferment at room temperature for about 4 hours. The sponge will rise and then fall; don't worry, this is normal.

Mixing and Kneading the Dough

Add the bread ingredients to the sponge, stirring until the dough forms a ball. Knead the dough for a total of about 10 minutes, letting yourself and the dough rest for 10 to 15 minutes in the middle. The dough should be smooth and a little tacky but not too sticky.

Fermenting the Dough

Put the dough into your dough-rising bucket and put the lid on, or put it back in the mixing bowl and cover the bowl with plastic wrap. Let the dough ferment at room temperature till it doubles, about 90 minutes.

Shaping and Proofing the Dough

Form the dough into a loaf to fit the bread pan. Lightly grease the loaf pan and place the shaped dough into the pan. Cover it loosely with plastic wrap and let proof for 60 to 90 minutes; it should about double

TIP

Rye dough should be kneaded less than wheat dough. If kneading in a mixer, knead at low speed so gluten strands don't break.

in volume, with the top of the loaf forming a dome shape but not over-flowing the sides of the pan.

Baking the Bread

Preheat your oven to 350°F (176°C). Bake the bread for 45 to 55 minutes; it should look evenly colored and sound hollow when tapped on the bottom of the loaf. Transfer the loaf to a cooling rack. Leave it in the pan for a few minutes before tipping it out onto the rack. Let the loaf cool for at least 90 minutes before slicing.

Variation: Sourdough Rye Bread

This is a very simple variation on the yeasted rye bread recipe above. We're just substituting a refreshed levain or barm starter for the sponge and eliminating the yeast. Note that you're refreshing the starter with a good proportion of rye flour, and more water than usual,

FIGURE 17.1. Freshly baked, aromatic rye bread.

too; rye ferments very quickly, and a little thinner consistency to the starter just helps the process along, especially in cold weather.

Timing

- 3 to 5 minutes to refresh starter
- 8 to 12 hours to ferment starter
- 10 to 25 minutes to mix and knead dough
- 8 to 12 hours to ferment dough
- 60 to 90 minutes to shape and proof dough
- 45 to 55 minutes to bake

Equipment you'll definitely need

- Small mixing bowl for refreshing starter
- Large mixing bowl (stainless steel, glass, Pyrex, or ceramic)
- Wooden spoon and wire whisk
- Large wooden cutting board
- Standard bread loaf pan

Stuff that's not absolutely necessary but recommended

- Kitchen scale
- 2-quart dough-rising bucket

Starter ingredients	Metric	US	Baker's %
• Storage levain or barm	about 50 to 100 g	¼ to ½ cup	38 to 76
• Rye flour, preferably stone-ground	65 g	½ cup	50
• Unbleached bread flour	65 g	½ cup	50
• Unchlorinated water, cool	236	1 cup	181

Bread ingredients	Metric	US	Baker's %
• Unbleached bread flour	275 g	2 cups	100
• Sea salt	7 g	1¼ tsp	2
• SAF or other instant yeast	1.5 g	½ tsp	0.6
• Caraway seeds	9 g	1 Tbsp	3.8
• Milk or buttermilk	57 g	¼ cup	24

Refresh Your Starter

About 8 to 12 hours before you want to mix up your bread dough, refresh the starter. In a small mixing bowl, to stir all the sponge ingredients together with a wooden spoon or wire whisk to make a smooth batter. Cover the bowl with plastic wrap and ferment at room temperature for 8 to 12 hours.

Mixing and Kneading the Dough

Scrape the refreshed levain into a large mixing bowl. Add the bread ingredients to the starter, stirring until the dough forms a ball. Knead the dough for a total of about 10 minutes, letting yourself and the dough rest for 10 to 15 minutes in the middle. The dough should be smooth and a little tacky but not too sticky.

Fermenting the Dough

Put the dough into your dough-rising bucket and put the lid on, or put it back in the mixing bowl and cover the bowl with plastic wrap. Let the dough ferment at cool room temperature till it doubles, about 8 hours or overnight.

Shaping and Proofing the Dough

Form the dough into a loaf to fit the bread pan. Lightly grease the pan and place the dough in it. Cover loosely with plastic wrap and let proof for 60 to 90 minutes; it might not double in volume, but it should just about fill the pan; the top will begin forming a dome shape.

Baking the Bread

Preheat your oven to 350°F (176°C). Bake the bread for 45 to 55 minutes; it should look evenly colored and sound hollow when tapped on the bottom. Transfer the loaf to a cooling rack. Leave it in the pan for a few minutes before tipping it out onto the rack. Cool for at least 90 minutes before slicing.

SEXY SCIENCE TALK

How Making Rye Bread Will Help You Make Gluten-free Bread

Rye proteins can't form an elastic gluten network, apparently because their glutenin molecules are unable to link up into end-to-end chains. So rye breads depend more on the starches in the grain to provide the structure of the bread; the acidity of fast-fermenting rye dough helps limit starch breakdown and also makes the dough more elastic.

So…if you're interested in baking with less gluten, or even avoiding gluten altogether, try baking with rye flour first. Because of the smallish amount of gluten in rye, it will give you a chance to get used to working with low- to no-gluten grains and the differences in how the dough is mixed, fermented, and baked. To ease yourself into it, just substitute rye flour for some of the wheat flour in any yeast bread recipe. When you're ready, check out Chapter 18 to get more in depth with low- and no-gluten baking.

PART FIVE

LOW– AND NO–GLUTEN BREADS

Comfort Zone 6:
Low- and No-gluten Breads

Bear with me; I'm going to be repeating some information from Chapter 4 about gluten. Just in case you skipped that chapter, or you aren't convinced that wheat or other gluten grains are safe to eat, please do consider the following discussion.

Low-gluten and Low-wheat Baking

As mentioned earlier, if you have celiac disease, you must avoid all gluten. In recent years, gluten has become the scapegoat for a laundry list of human ailments, spawning a multi-billion-dollar industry of gluten-free products. The manufacturers, for the most part, have made little effort to educate the public about gluten. Many people don't even know what gluten is; I've heard of bottled water and even watermelons being labeled gluten-free. The fact is, gluten exists in three grains: wheat, rye, and barley. Of these, wheat has significantly larger amounts of gluten than the others.

I am frequently asked if it's true that sourdough starter (a culture of wild yeasts and lactobacillus bacteria used to leaven baked goods) somehow inactivates the gluten in wheat flour. A number of studies suggest this is true; in controlled lab conditions, bread dough inoculated with certain strains of lactobacillus and then fermented for many hours has been shown to indicate much lower levels of gluten than before fermentation. These studies all conclude that more research is needed, however.

If you think you are sensitive to gluten, you might actually be react-
ing to something else in wheat. Wheat prolamins and fructose, as well
as other carbohydrates found in wheat and other grains, are all known
to cause digestive issues in some people. (See sidebar in Chapter 4 on
FODMAPs and fructose malabsorption.)

Recent research suggests that many people who have trouble di-
gesting wheat (or other grains) have fewer symptoms when the grain
is consumed in smaller quantities. Gluten (and other components of
wheat to which some people are sensitive) is digested in the small intestine; however, the gut can absorb only a limited amount of these
molecules at one time. When consumed in typical American-sized portions, things like wheat bread and pasta can cause bloating, gas, and diarrhea in sensitive individuals. That's because once the small intestine
has reached the limit of its gluten-digesting capacity, the excess travels
to the large intestine, which isn't designed to digest it, resulting in gas,
bloating, etc., symptoms often blamed on gluten but possibly caused by
other components of wheat.

Why not try lowering your wheat intake, rather than giving up on
it altogether? One strategy would be to simply reduce the portion size,
limiting the amount of wheat being digested at any one time. I am testing bread recipes that have greatly reduced amounts of wheat; these
breads are made largely of gluten-free grains, with just enough wheat
flour to enable them to rise and have a pleasing texture. For example, I
have successfully made bread using gluten-free grains but with added
wheat-based sourdough starter. With the right proportion of this
starter, the bread rises nicely and has a soft, chewy texture, but with
much less gluten and fructose than comparable all-wheat bread.

If you feel better when you aren't eating wheat, don't eat it. This is
a quality-of-life question, and I want you to enjoy your food and not
unnecessarily risk discomfort. But if you are not sure if you're intol-
erant of wheat or gluten, consider lowering your wheat intake, either
by reducing portion sizes or substituting gluten-free grains for wheat
when you bake. You might discover that you can enjoy wheat products
again, in moderation, if you listen to your gut and learn to work with it.

Lowering Your Gluten Intake by Varying Grains

Softer wheat like **all-purpose flour** may be easier to digest for people who are sensitive to wheat or gluten.

Barley contains significant quantities (about 5% of the grain weight) of two carbohydrates other than starch: pentosans (which make rye flour sticky) and glucans (which give oats its gelatinous and cholesterol-lowering qualities). Along with barley's water-insoluble proteins, these carbohydrates contribute to the springy texture of cooked grains. Barley absorbs twice as much water as wheat, so you'll want to adjust the hydration rate of your dough.

Low- and No-gluten Baking Mixes

In the starter formulas below, I have aimed for at least 40% whole grains in the mix for added fiber. I'm calling these basic formulas because it is just a place to start; feel free to substitute other gluten-free grains for those listed, choosing from the list below. I haven't included rice flours in my mixes, just because I don't care for the taste of rice flour, and white rice flour has very little to recommend it nutritionally; brown rice flour at least offers some dietary fiber. Nut flours can be pretty pricey, but they do add considerable protein and fiber. Bob's Red Mill makes a garbanzo-fava bean flour mix called Gar-Fava.

FIGURE 18.1. A variety of gluten-free flours.

Some sources I have looked at advocate mixes with 30% whole-grain flours and 70% starch flours. The idea is that this ratio mimics the ratio of starch to protein and fiber in wheat. Actually, wheat is about 20% protein and 70% starch, and the rest is fiber, water, fat, and minerals. I'm not sure why trying to keep to this ratio is preferable in gluten-free mixes. Most of the starch-type flours are very highly processed, and break down into sugars very rapidly in your mouth when they come in contact with the amylase enzyme in saliva. The result is extremely rapid absorption of sugar into the bloodstream, just like with highly processed wheat flour, leading to blood sugar spikes that strain the pancreas and generally mess about with metabolism.

Whole-grain GF flours	White GF flours and starches	Nut flours	Bean flours
Brown rice flour	Arrowroot flour	Almond flour	Fava bean flour
Buckwheat flour	Cornstarch	Chestnut flour	Garbanzo bean flour
Corn flour	Potato flour	Coconut flour	Kinako (roasted soy bean) flour
Millet flour	Potato starch	Hazelnut flour	
Oat flour	Sweet rice flour		
Quinoa flour	Tapioca flour		
Sorghum flour	White rice flour		
Sweet potato flour			
Teff flour			

These formulas make 500 grams (1.1 pounds). If you want to mix up enough to store, it's very easy to double or triple these amounts; once again, measuring ingredients by weight just makes it all easier and more accurate. If you come up with a mix that you really like and want to give it away as gifts, take advantage of your knowledge of the baker's percentage (see Chapter 6 for a review) to make even larger quantities without struggling to do the math.

The gluten-free flours in the baking mix formulas here are all whole-grain flours, all fairly easy to find these days. Bob's Red Mill has quite a good selection, although they tend to be a little more expensive than buying in bulk; most are packaged in smallish bags, so they can be convenient when you're playing around with formulas.

Basic Formula: Low-gluten Baking Mix (makes 500 g)

Ingredients	Metric	US	Baker's %
• Unbleached all-purpose flour	100 g	about ¾ cup	20
• Whole wheat pastry flour	50 g	about ⅓ cup	10
• Oat flour	75 g	¾ cup	15
• Millet flour	200 g	1½ cups	40
• Quinoa flour	50 g	½ cup	10
• Teff flour	25 g	¼ cup	5

Basic formula: Whole-grain Gluten-free Baking Mix (makes 500 g)

Equipment you'll definitely need

• Large mixing bowl (stainless steel, glass, Pyrex, or ceramic)
• Wooden spoon
• Container with airtight lid for storing mix

Stuff that's not absolutely necessary but recommended

• Kitchen scale

Ingredients	Metric	US	Baker's %
• Oat flour	150 g	1½ cups	30
• Millet flour	225 g	1¾ cups	45
• Quinoa flour	100 g	1 cup	20
• Teff flour	25 g	¼ cup	5

SEXY SCIENCE TALK

Hydrolysis of Gluten in Low-wheat Sourdough Breads

This traditional fermentation process begins by "growing" strains of bacteria and yeast together in what bakers call the "starter." When the flour is then added to the starter, the organisms produce enzymes that act on the gluten protein, and thus hydrolysis begins. Hydrolysis is the breakdown of larger particles into smaller ones, specifically amino acids. These amino acids are no longer toxic to individuals who are sensitive to gluten.

A sourdough made from a mixture of wheat (30%) and non-toxic (gluten-free) oat, millet, and buckwheat flours was started with lactobacilli. After 24 hours of fermentation, wheat gliadins and low-molecular-mass, alcohol-soluble polypeptides were hydrolyzed almost totally.

A mixture of wheat, oat, millet, and buckwheat flours, at a ratio 3:1:4:2, was chosen as optimal for dough production. ("Sourdough Bread Made from Wheat and Nontoxic Flours and Started with Selected Lactobacilli Is Tolerated in Celiac Sprue Patient," *Applied and Environmental Microbiology*, 2004)

Gluten-free Yeast Breads

IF YOU'RE READING this chapter, you are no doubt aware that there are simply hordes of gluten-free recipes online, in books and magazines, and on gluten-free (GF) baking mix packages. What makes one gluten-free pizza recipe different from another? Mainly it comes down to what kinds of flours are used. Unlike most gluten-free bread recipes, my GF baking mix (see Chapter 18) contains no xanthan gum; based on results, I feel the oat flour's beta-glucans (which are what makes oatmeal seem a little gummy) accomplish the same effect as xanthan gum.

In my view, too many people are bound and determined to make some kind of gluten-free sandwich loaf that rivals the local bakery's artisan loaves. Keep your expectations realistic. Gluten-free bread is never going to be exactly like wheat bread; the lack of gluten makes that impossible. So let's do the best we can to make our gluten-free bread both tasty and nutritious, eh? Here's the thing: Gluten-free baking is much better suited to flatbreads like pizza, rolls, or any other bread that's not expected to rise all that much.

You'll notice that I have not included a lot of recipes here; plenty of good recipes are available in books and on the Internet. As with most of this book, my hope is to show you a jumping-off point as you move from one comfort zone to another. There are so many different ways of combining gluten-free flours to make breads…I can't tell you how to make one that fits your taste. Start with one of the recipes here or in another book or one you get from a friend or relative. It doesn't matter. But if you really want or need to minimize or eliminate gluten from your life, pick a place to begin and go for it. You may need to do some tweaking and experimenting, but keep in mind the big picture: your quality of life.

Here's a simple recipe for a gluten-free pizza crust.

 # Master Formula: Gluten-free Pizza

Timing

- 30 minutes to measure ingredients and mix dough
- 30 to 60 minutes to ferment the dough and prepare toppings
- 30 to 45 minutes to shape and proof dough
- 20 to 25 minutes to bake

Equipment you'll definitely need

- Small mixing bowl for yeast mixture
- Large mixing bowl (stainless steel, glass, Pyrex, or ceramic)
- Wooden spoon
- Wire whisk
- Parchment paper
- Baking sheet or pizza pan

Stuff that's not absolutely necessary but recommended

- Kitchen scale

Ingredients	Metric	US	Baker's %
• Unchlorinated water, warm	350 g	1½ cups	65
• SAF or other instant yeast	6 g	1½ tsp	1.2
• Extra-virgin olive oil	30 g	2 Tbsp	6
• Gluten-free baking mix*	500 g	4 cups	100
• Buttermilk powder or dry milk powder	35 g	¼ cup	7
• Baking powder	8 g	2 tsp	1.6
• Sea salt	10 g	1½ tsp	2

* Use basic gluten-free baking mix, a commercial GF baking mix, or your own blend (see Chapter 18). Note that the amount of water listed is for the basic gluten-free baking mix; other blends may need more or less water, as some grains absorb more water than others.

Mixing the Dough

Stir the baking mix, buttermilk or dry milk powder, baking powder, and salt in a large mixing bowl to blend.

In a small bowl, combine the warm water, yeast, and olive oil; whisk in about 65 g (½ cup) of the dry ingredient mix. Blend it thoroughly, but don't worry if there are a few lumps. Let this mixture rest for 20 to 30 minutes; it will look bubbly and smell pleasantly yeasty.

Add the yeast mixture to the dry ingredients. If you're using a stand mixer, mix on medium-high speed (8 on a KitchenAid mixer) for 3 to 4 minutes. If mixing by hand, a whisk works better than a wooden spoon, although whisking definitely takes more muscle. Your dough should be smooth, thick, and sticky; it has no gluten, so it won't feel stretchy like wheat dough.

Fermenting the Dough

Cover the bowl with plastic wrap or a clean kitchen towel and let it rest for 30 to 60 minutes at room temperature. This is a good time to organize and prepare any toppings you want for your pizza.

Shaping and Baking the Bread

Preheat your oven to 425°F (218°C). Lightly oil your baking sheet with olive oil, or cover the baking sheet with a piece of parchment paper. Either way, you can dust the baking sheet with coarse cornmeal if you like.

Divide the dough in half, and put one portion in the middle of the baking sheet. Use your fingers, dipping them in cool water as needed to prevent sticking, to shape the dough, starting at

---

SEXY SCIENCE TALK

Using Chemical Leavening with Gluten-free Doughs

Comparatively weak doughs such as rye and gluten-free doughs can't hold gas bubbles for more than a few minutes, so a faster-acting source of gas than yeast is helpful. Especially if you are using a low- or no-gluten sourdough starter, adding a chemical leavener like baking soda will improve results. The reaction between the acid in the starter and the alkaline of the baking soda produces CO_2.

As a general rule, 2 g (½ teaspoon) of baking soda is neutralized by 240ml (1 cup) soured milk, 5ml (1 teaspoon) lemon juice or vinegar, or 5 g (1¼ teaspoons) cream of tartar.

Double-acting baking powder inflates one set of bubbles when mixed in a batter and another set during baking.

The gluten-free pizza recipe above includes baking powder. If possible, I highly recommend using aluminum-free baking powder.

the center and working outward to form a circle, oval, or rectangle. Let the dough rest uncovered for 15 to 30 minutes.

Bake for 8 to 10 minutes, just until set. Take it out of the oven and add your toppings. Return the pan to the oven, and continue baking for 10 to 15 minutes, depending on what toppings you use.

Variation: Seeded Gluten-free Dinner Rolls

Follow the recipe above for Gluten-free Pizza. At least 8 hours before you mix your dough, put about ⅓ cup (total) of your choice of seeds—flax, sunflower, sesame (or some of each, my favorite)—in a small bowl. Stir in ½ cup rolled oats. Add enough cool water to cover by at least ½ inch. Let soak for at least 8 hours.

If any water hasn't been soaked up by the seeds and oats, drain the mixture in a strainer. Add the seeds to the yeast mixture just before adding the dry ingredients.

Let the dough ferment for at least 1 hour at room temperature. Preheat your oven to 350°F (176°C). Lay a piece of parchment paper on a baking sheet. Use your hands to scoop up about ½ cup of the dough and gently shape it into a roll. It helps to wear nitrile gloves and dip your hands in cool water, as the dough will be sticky. Try not to handle the dough more than necessary, to avoid bursting gas bubbles. Put the roll on the parchment, and continue shaping rolls, spacing them about 2" apart.

Cover the rolls with plastic wrap and let rest about 30 minutes. Bake for 25 to 30 minutes. Transfer to cooling rack and let cool for at least 15 minutes.

Gluten-free Sourdough Starters and Breads

ANOTHER FREQUENTLY asked question: Can I make a gluten-free sourdough starter? Answer: absolutely. I've done it many times, using commercial GF baking mixes as well as my own formulas. There's no real trick to it; just substitute your own GF baking mix (or one or more of the gluten-free flours listed above) for the flours in the levain or barm methods in Chapter 14.

Why bother? Well, I know from experience that gluten-free breads made using a sourdough starter rise a little better and have a more pleasing texture. I may not understand all the reasons why this is true, but since I've consistently had similar results, I believe it makes a difference. (I suspect that if I spent more time studying the phenomenon of sourdough rye breads, I would get a clue or two on this, but so far I just haven't taken the time.)

Although any of the gluten-free flours can be used separately or in combination to create a starter, here are a few tips:

* Use at least a little whole-grain flour. Whole grains have minerals that feed the yeast.
* **Teff flour** ferments very rapidly, so just a little added to your starter will speed up the fermentation process, just like rye flour does in a wheat-based starter.
* Use enough water to make a slightly runny consistency, especially when you are first cultivating the starter. It will ferment a little more quickly than a stiffer mix.

* Coconut flour absorbs 4 times its weight in liquid. Hydration rates can vary a lot from one kind of flour to another. I would give your starter a stir 30 to 60 minutes after you add water to it; if it looks a lot thicker, it's because the flour has absorbed a lot of the water. No worries; just add a little more water and keep an eye on it until it has the consistency you want.

* The starter won't have the same consistency as wheat-based starter, since there is no gluten to make it stretchy. Once the yeast is actively reproducing, though, it will start to appear bubbly and will increase in volume as the gas bubbles expand.

Making a Gluten-free Sourdough Starter

Just in case you skipped the chapter on making your own sourdough starter and went right to the gluten-free stuff, here's how you make that starter. Please note that it may take a little longer than four days to activate this starter, depending on what kind of flours you use, the temperature in your kitchen, and other variables. Be patient; I promise you the wild yeast is there and will respond to your ministrations. This really does work.

You will need

- A medium-sized mixing bowl
- A 1-quart clear container, with a lid. I like the dough-rising buckets from King Arthur Flour, which come in several sizes. A wide-mouth Mason jar will work too, although I find a wider, shorter container makes it easier to add and mix ingredients.

Day 1

- Pour into a bowl: 75 g (⅓ cup) tepid spring water.
- Stir in 100 g (⅔ cup) basic gluten-free baking mix, another GF baking mix, or any combination of gluten-free flours you prefer (see

Chapter 18). Stir till all the flour has been moistened, adding a little water if needed. Dough will be sticky.

- Cover the bowl with plastic wrap and let it stand at room temperature for 24 hours.

Day 2

- The culture will look much the same as on Day 1, although it may have risen slightly.
- Add 30 g (2 tablespoons) tepid spring water and 50 g (⅓ cup) gluten-free baking mix or flours of your choice.
- Stir to blend. If needed, add a little more water and stir to incorporate all the flour.
- Cover the bowl with plastic wrap, and let stand at room temperature for 24 hours.

Day 3

- Your culture will have expanded 1½ to 2 times its original volume. You should see bubbles forming below the surface, and the smell will be slightly yeasty and fruity.
- Repeat feeding steps of Day 2, cover, and let stand at room temperature for 24 hours.

Day 4 and on

- Your starter may be ready to use any time in the next few days. When it's ready, you will observe most or all of the following:
  - Surface of culture looks dimpled or bubbly and may rise to a dome.
  - Smells like ripe, slightly sour fruit and tastes tangy or acidic, like citrus fruit.

✷ T I P ✷

Because some flours absorb a lot more water than others, consider the amount of water specified in the various steps below a guideline; it's important that all the flour in the starter is well hydrated. So start by stirring in enough water to get all the flour good and wet. Then let it sit for a few minutes, and check it again; you want to end up with a slightly runny mix, like thick pancake batter. Don't be afraid to add more water; it's better to be a little wetter than a little too dry.

✷ T I P ✷

Once your starter is cultivated, active, and bubbly, please keep it in the fridge! At room temperature or warmer, the starter will ferment much more quickly, requiring frequent refreshment in order to avoid excessive acid buildup. The cool temperature in your refrigerator won't kill those yeasts, I promise; they simply work at a more leisurely pace. When you take the starter out to refresh or use it, you will see that it has increased in volume.

- If it doesn't already look like this, simply repeat Day 3 steps until it does.
- Transfer starter to 1 quart container and put on lid.
- Store starter in refrigerator, and refresh once a week by following Day 2 steps.

Injera

Here is a recipe for injera, a gluten-free flatbread from Ethiopia. It is a soft, spongy bread, almost like a large pancake, made with teff flour. I remember being fascinated by injera (not that I knew its name at the time) at a wonderful Ethiopian restaurant in Seattle many years ago. I learned how to eat it by surreptitiously glancing at other diners, who were calmly tearing off pieces and using it to pick up pieces of meat and eat it all with their fingers. The injera was like a large spongy, delightfully tangy pancake, and it was a lot of fun wrapping it around food and eating the whole meal with my fingers.

The batter is made several days ahead of time, fermenting and becoming quite sour before the bread is cooked. You can speed up the process a bit by adding yeast if you want; I've found that teff ferments very quickly on its own, though, so it's up to you. Traditionally injera is cooked on a large earthenware pan, but I have had good results using a 12" cast-iron skillet. You can also use a large non-stick pan; I prefer cast-iron or stainless steel pans, although electric fry pans work very well, too.

Timing

- 3 to 5 minutes to measure ingredients and mix batter
- 2 to 3 days to ferment batter
- 30 minutes to proof dough
- 3 to 5 minutes to bake each injera; recipe makes 7 or 8 10"- to 12"-diameter breads

Equipment you'll definitely need

- Large mixing bowl (stainless steel, glass, Pyrex, or ceramic)
- Wire whisk
- Medium saucepan
- Ladle
- Large (12″ diameter is ideal) cast-iron, stainless steel, or non-stick skillet with lid
- Large spatula
- Clean kitchen towel

Stuff that's not absolutely necessary but recommended

- Kitchen scale
- Electric fry pan (optional but nice)

Ingredients	Metric	US	Baker's %
• Unchlorinated water, lukewarm	350 g	1½ cups	152
• Teff flour, finely ground	230 g	2 cups	100
• SAF or other instant yeast (optional)	4 g	1 tsp	1.7

Mixing the Batter

Put the teff flour in a large mixing bowl. Stir in 591 g (2½ cups) luke-warm water, whisking to break up lumps. If using yeast, dissolve it in the remaining 118 g (½ cup) warm water and stir into the batter. Cover the bowl, and let rest at room temperature for 2 or 3 days to ferment and sour. It will not increase noticeably in volume, but it will be bubbly and smell and taste quite sour.

Making the Injera

If any liquid has separated from the batter and is floating on top, drain it off carefully. In a saucepan, bring 236 g (1 cup) water to a boil. Stir in about 130 g (½ cup) of the batter, whisking to blend. Reduce heat to medium and cook, stirring, until it has thickened. Remove from heat, and cool until warm but not hot. Stir into the rest of the batter. The batter should be fairly runny, like thin pancake batter; add a little water if needed to thin it out a bit. Let the batter ferment for at least 30 minutes, up to an hour.

Preheat your skillet over medium heat; if you're using an electric fry pan, heat it to 420°F (215°C). When the pan is hot, stir the batter and scoop about ½ cup of it in a large ladle. Working quickly, pour it into the hot pan, using a circular motion starting from the outside of the pan and toward the center. Tilt the pan if you need to, to fill in any empty spots.

Cover and cook for 2 minutes; when ready to turn, the edges of the batter will be pulling away from the sides of the pan, and the surface of the injera will look bubbly. If it's not quite done, wipe condensation off the lid, cover the pan again, and cook another minute or two.

Use the spatula to lift the injera from the pan, transferring it to a clean kitchen towel. Wrap the towel over the injera to keep it warm and moist while you cook the rest of the injera.

Besan Roti (Chickpea Country Bread)

I adore Indian foods of all kinds, and in my spare time this year, I've been learning a few things about Indian cooking. It's been very interesting to see the differences in foods from region to region; I also had no idea how much wheat and other grains are grown in India. Chapter 24 has a recipe for traditional Indian naan, one of the best breads ever, in my opinion. Here is my gluten-free version of besan roti, a country bread from northwestern India. My take on this bread involves using your gluten-free sourdough starter, so be sure you have that on hand before beginning. Although this bread is essentially unleavened, I like the addition of the starter and a short fermentation time because it enhances the flavor of the bread.

Besan roti is delicious served with a curry dish of your choice. It is a lot like a fresh tortilla, but with an unmistakable Indian accent. It is traditionally baked in a hot oven, but I get good results cooking it like a flour tortilla, on a cast-iron griddle on the gas stove. Like the injera above, besan roti can also be cooked in an electric fry pan.

Timing

- 8 hours or more to refresh sourdough
- 5 to 10 minutes to prep and measure ingredients
- 40 to 70 minutes to mix and ferment dough
- 30 to 40 minutes to shape and rest dough
- 10 minutes to roll out breads
- 2 to 3 minutes to bake each bread; recipe makes 8 breads about 8" in diameter

Equipment you'll definitely need

- Large mixing bowl (stainless steel, glass, Pyrex, or ceramic)
- Wire whisk and wooden spoon
- Rolling pin
- Large cutting board or clean counter surface
- Large skillet, griddle, or electric frypan
- Large spatula
- Clean kitchen towel

Stuff that's not absolutely necessary but recommended

- Kitchen scale
- Food processor

Ingredients	Metric	US	Baker's %
• Small onion, finely minced		1	
• Whole cumin seed	about 3 g	1 tsp	1.3
• Chickpea (garbanzo bean) flour	95 g	1 cup	40
• Sea salt	3.5 g	½ tsp	1.5
• Vegetable oil or peanut oil	28 g	2 Tbsp	12
• Unchlorinated water	118 g	½ cup	51
• Basic gluten-free baking mix (see Chapter 18)	about 135 g	1 cup	60
• Gluten-free sourdough starter, refreshed (see below)	90 g	½ cup	39

Refreshing the Sourdough Starter

About 8 hours before you plan to mix your dough, refresh the starter. Scoop about 45 g (¼ cup) of your gluten-free starter into a small bowl. Refresh it by adding 14 g (2 teaspoons) teff flour and 18 g (2 tablespoons) gluten-free baking mix, plus enough cool water to make a thick batter. Cover and let ferment at room temperature for at least 8 hours.

Mixing the Batter

If you're using a food processor, process the chopped onion and cumin seed until the onion is very finely chopped. Add the chickpea flour, salt, and oil, processing for another 25 to 30 seconds. Add the water gradually, with the motor running. Leave the batter in the processor, and let it rest for 15 minutes.

If not using a food processor, mince the onion as finely as you can. Crush the cumin seed slightly in a mortar and pestle or spice grinder, then blend with the onion in a mixing bowl.

Add the baking mix to the chickpea flour mixture, and stir (or process) until a dough forms. Add the starter, and stir another 2 minutes (or process 45 seconds). Turn the dough out onto a lightly floured surface (you can use any gluten-free flour), and knead the dough briefly. Put the dough back in the mixing bowl, cover, and let ferment for 30 to 60 minutes.

Dividing and Shaping the Dough

Divide the dough into 8 pieces. Flour your hands, and pat each piece into a round about 3" or 4" in diameter. Set them aside, but don't stack them; they will stick together.

Rolling and Baking the Breads

Preheat your skillet, griddle, or electric fry pan to medium-high heat, 420° (215°C) in an electric fry pan. Roll out each round to a thin tortilla-like shape about 8" in diameter. The dough is fragile and will tear easily, so flour your rolling pin as needed.

As each bread is rolled out, lift it carefully onto your skillet, griddle, or fry pan. Bake for about 2 minutes; you'll see tiny bubbles forming over the whole surface of the bread. It will look pale yellow on top, and the bottom will have brown flecks like flour tortillas. When baked, lift it with a spatula onto a clean kitchen towel, wrapping it to keep warm while the other breads are baked.

Variation: Low-gluten Besan Roti

Try using whole-wheat pastry flour in place of the gluten-free baking mix in this recipe. The taste and texture will be slightly different but closer to the traditional besan roti and relatively low in gluten.

What Will You Do with *Your* Gluten-free Sourdough Starter?

I hope you're beginning to get an idea of just how versatile your gluten-free sourdough starter can be. If you can allow yourself to set aside the notion that all bread has to be in a sandwich-shaped loaf, you'll discover a whole world (literally) of amazing breads that can be made with grains that have little or no gluten. The sourdough starter really does make a difference in the texture and flavor of bread, including gluten-free breads.

Have fun and experiment! Add some sourdough starter to any gluten-free yeast bread, and compare results for yourself. When you feel comfortable with it, eliminate the yeast, and leaven your bread using only your starter; you'll have to increase the fermentation time, but you'll figure it out. Now you know one of my secrets: Instead of buying more books or looking up more recipes on the Internet, just take recipes you already have and make substitutions. Do keep notes, though; sooner or later you'll come up with something incredibly yummy, and you'll want to be able to duplicate it.

PART SIX

THE WOOD-FIRED OVEN

The Homestead Hearth:
Why and How I Built
My Wood-fired Oven

Three scents accompany my memories of this place:
Cut wood, poppy-seed bread, and the soft, crisp smell of snow.
— Elif Shafak

An outdoor bread oven had been on David's wish list since before I met him in 1999. Years ago, while sharing a house in Seattle with some college students, he was regularly baking whole-grain bread, using the sponge method. Over the years, he had seen wood-fired ovens in various restaurants, and that sparked his interest.

Before we moved to the farm in 2006, we had talked about building a wood-fired oven someday. I didn't actually start putting that plan into action until the summer of 2015; up to that point, our priorities were getting the solar electric system up and running, operating our small farm business, and looking after our chickens, turkeys, ducks, and pigs. After my first time speaking at the Mother Earth News Fair in 2011, I was also spending more time traveling to these events, and then starting to write books. So the dream of having our own outdoor bread oven was on hold for quite a while.

In July 2015, after a lot of research and planning, we chose a spot for the oven, and I started in on the project.

Why was having a wood-fired bread oven important to us? Well, by this time I had been fairly seriously studying bread-making in general and sourdough in particular. One of my main resources was *The Bread*

183

FIGURE 21.1. My nearly finished outdoor oven.

Builders (see Appendix B), still considered by many to be the bible of artisan bread-making. Not only does this book delve deeply into the science and craft of bread-making, it also has a section on wood-fired ovens, including plans for a large brick oven. That was what really got me interested in wood-fired ovens and hearth baking, although there was no way I could afford to build that kind of brick oven, even if I had the requisite masonry skills to do it.

What also motivated both of us was the thought of being able to bake bread (and presumably cook other things as well) using less fossil fuel. We heat our off-grid home with two woodstoves and have plenty of potential oven fuel here in the woods. It's also great to be able to bake bread, even in the hottest part of the summer, without heating up the house or having to get up at some ungodly hour to bake while the house is still cool.

Pioneers and homesteaders used their wood-fired ovens for a lot more than just cooking and baking. Pasteurizing milk, sterilizing feathers from homestead flocks before using them to make pillows and mattresses, cooking whole meals—these are just a few of the ways they learned to use their ovens. Often at the end of a long day of baking and cooking, the waning heat of the oven was the perfect place to stuff more wood to dry out in preparation for the next time the oven was fired up.

Building the Oven

After more research, and a whole lot of sketching and calculating on a notepad, I decided I was ready to have at it. One of my plans was to use only materials found on the property, at least as much as possible. Partly this was an economic issue, just trying to minimize the cash outlay; also, I more or less expected I would be writing about that project someday, and I believed this approach would appeal to my intended audience.

Of our two large ponds on the property, one has a large natural clay deposit, fortunately located on the near shore and easy to access. Having decided to build my oven using a mixture of clay and sand, I thought it would be a simple matter to dig the clay I needed, haul it to the oven site, mix it with sand and water, and, you know, build the oven. It would be fun, I thought. And easy! Ah, the innocence of middle age.

FIGURE 21.2. Clay from a deposit near the pond; it will be mixed with sand and water to make cob.

Design Points

First of all, I am not going to teach you how to build your own clay oven. For one thing, I've done it exactly once; I'm no expert. And there are good books out there, including the ones I used as my main resources for planning (see Appendix B), that will guide you. I will, however, share a few lessons I learned along the way; ideas that occurred to me that have worked out well and others I would definitely do differently if I should ever build another similar oven.

How Tall Should the Oven Be?

One of the major decisions I made was the height of the oven. I have seen many pictures of beautiful clay ovens, sculpted like animals, birds, and dragons; quite a few of them had hearths that were inches off the ground. Even for someone much younger than me, I can't imagine it being easy or comfortable to be down on hands and knees every time to add fuel or put in or take out bread. I certainly haven't seen any photos of such ovens with happy, smiling bakers actually using them, crouching down, looking like they're enjoying themselves.

No doubt ovens like these are faster to build and involve much less material, but I'm really glad I decided to build this oven at a comfortable working height. I read that a standard working height for the top of the hearth is 40", so I planned my oven with that in mind. Another advantage is the large amount of thermal mass under a hearth of this height; this oven, which isn't all that big really, has between 5,000 and 6,000 pounds of clay, rock, and sand under the hearth. It takes a while for the hearth to get good and hot, but once it does heat up, it stays hot for 2 days (longer in summer).

Location

I wasn't certain where the oven would be located until I was just about ready to start building. The space we chose is limited in size, partly by trees and berry bushes. Because we live in the mountains, I had decided to lay a deep foundation of drain rock under the oven to prevent frost heave in winter. I staked out the foundation hole at about 8' by 8' and went from there. Since I wanted the drain rock to extend outside the oven walls by at least 18", it was easy to lay out the maximum size of the oven using an old piece of garden hose.

Oven Size

Then I just had to do the math: I wanted a certain dome thickness, as well as a good thick layer of insulation over the dome, so I sketched this out on paper too. The hearth size (inside dimensions) is about 42" front to back and 28" side to side. It's not huge but plenty big to bake a lot of bread or pizza at once.

One of the first questions I get about this oven is, Can you bake anything but pizza in this thing? Absolutely. While planning, I figured I was going to be putting a lot of time and effort and materials into the project (little did I know), so it made sense to me to make the oven, and the doorway, big enough to be able to cook a variety of things. As it turns out, it is plenty big enough to cook a whole tom turkey!

Judging Oven Temperature

One of my main questions, and the cause of most of my steep learning curve with this oven, was how do I know the temperature in there? Several books suggested tossing a handful of flour onto the hearth; the theory is that you time how long it takes for the flour to turn brown, and that lets you estimate the temperature. One actually suggested sticking your arm in there; I can only say I do **not** recommend that. Yow.

I decided to embed several thermocouples at various places as I was building, which involved more necessary learning on my part. The hearth bricks are laid before the oven dome is built, so first I drilled a hole in one of the hearth bricks, roughly in the center of the hearth, and cemented in a thermocouple. These are nice stainless-steel thermocouples with long braided wires; I ran the wires through ⅛" copper tubing that is embedded in the clay from the thermocouples out to the thermometer they are attached to. There are three thermocouples: one in the hearth brick, one a few inches deep in the clay at the top of the dome, and one in the clay at the back of the dome. The thermometer they are plugged into shows all three temperatures at once.

It's incredibly helpful to be able to see these temperatures, especially in the hearth. But what I don't know with any accuracy is what the *air* temperature is in there. I have figured out, through a lot of trial and error (mostly error), when the best time is to put in loaf bread, by watching the hearth temperature. Before I sorted this out, I had my share of loaves that looked good, or sometimes fairly black, on the out-

FIGURE 21.3. First thermocouple in place in sub-floor; it will be cemented into a hole drilled in a hearth brick.

FIGURE 21.4. Thermometer connected to thermocouples shows real-time temperatures in the hearth, the top and back of the oven dome.

side but were basically raw inside. The same thing happened the first couple of times I cooked whole chickens.

I have tried to keep notes as I've been learning to cook in this oven, but I haven't been very consistent about it. Some things I tend to remember better than others when it comes to cooking and baking with wood heat. But I tell you what, although I don't eat pizza very often, and am fairly picky about it when I do, I have been completely blown away by the pizza this oven turns out. My best guess (short of installing a fourth strategic thermocouple) is that when I put pizza in there, it is somewhere around 900°F (482°C); 12" Neapolitan pizzas (see Chapter 13) cook beautifully in barely 90 seconds. I am fortunate to have avoided singing my hair the first few times I used this oven; the fast-moving air coming out that door is unbelievably hot.

Advantages of the Wood-fired Oven

This kind of oven has a big advantage over our kitchen oven. Its heat is of all three kinds: conduction, convection, and radiation. The shape of the oven, as well as the height of the dome relative to the height of the door, all factor into how efficiently the oven heats up.

I've read quite a bit about the traditional outdoor bread ovens of Quebec. What researchers discovered, after visiting many of these oven sites, was that in the most efficient ovens, there was an optimum ratio between the door height and the dome height. The idea is that the oven door is about 63% of the inside height of the dome. Get this ratio right, and the oven is super-efficient. Here's how it works.

Once a small fire is burning on the hearth, inside the door, the airflow created by the heat of the fire draws cool air in through the door, down low on the hearth. This cool air travels straight back over the hearth, warming up as it goes through the fire. Then it follows the curve of the dome, picking up speed as it heats up even more, and rushes back out at the top of the door. This is the convection action that quickly heats up my oven to 800° to 900°F (426° to 482°C).

Having built a brick archway for my oven door before building the dome, I planned the height of the dome based on the finished height

FIGURE 21.5. Tandoor meal cooked in the outdoor oven.

of the door. I ended up with a door height of about 10" and an inside dome height of 16", pretty close to the ideal ratio.

Beyond Wood-fired Pizza

I have had plenty of other ideas about how to use this oven. While looking at the oven one day, it occurred to me that it resembled a tandoor oven laid on its side. (OK, so it looks more like a slightly melted miniature igloo.) This past year or so, I've been learning something about Indian cooking, so I was excited about trying some Indian dishes in the oven. They say that somehow the clay walls and dome of the oven add their own flavor to the food, adding a little mystique to the process.

I made a traditional tandoor meal of tandoori chicken, naan bread, and salat (a traditional vegetable salad). I marinated two whole chickens in a heavily spiced, yogurt-based marinade, then roasted them in the wood-fired oven. This first attempt wasn't quite perfect; I probably put the chicken in a little too soon, when the oven was too hot. The skin was fairly charred, but the meat was perfectly cooked, tender and juicy and so flavorful! By the time the chicken came out of the oven, the temperature had dropped enough that I thought it was safe to bake the naan. This was the first time I had ever made naan, so I was unreasonably pleased when it baked beautifully on the first try.

So far, I've cooked and baked a lot of different things in this oven but haven't very often attempted to cook a whole meal. It's certainly an organizational challenge, planning the cooking sequence. But gosh, the results! And it seems to me that our pioneer ancestors managed this on a daily basis, with fewer resources than I have.

Who knows, there might just be a way to turn this whole project into some kind of new farm enterprise. Once I've reached a level of some proficiency with this wood-fired oven, I think it would be fun to teach classes. Wood-fired pizza is so popular these days, I could keep busy just hosting pizza parties. When I have time to get to my forge, I'd like to custom-make a spit roaster for my oven, which will certainly make it easier to cook things like tandoori chicken.

If you do decide to build your own wood-fired oven, don't limit yourself to pizza. I know a few people who built ovens with very low domes, specifically designed for pizza; they work great, but every one of those people ended up wishing they could cook something other than pizza, simply because the results are so amazing.

It took me quite a while to build my oven, but it was entirely worth the time and effort. I learned a lot and built something useful that will last a good long time. Oh, and I got to check one more thing off the wish list!

Heating and Using Your Wood-fired Oven

What Kind of Wood Do I Use for Fuel?

As I said, we're fortunate to live on wooded land that provides us with more than enough fuel to heat our home. We go to quite a bit of work to cut firewood and split and stack it before the cold weather sets in. It was quite a revelation to me to discover that some of the best oven fuel can be made from the branches of the trees we cut for heating.

Cutting down trees, regardless of your skill or experience, is a very dangerous operation. All sorts of things can go wrong: A slight breeze just when a tree starts to fall can push it in an unexpected direction; the falling tree can knock branches off adjacent trees as it comes down; the trunk can jackknife backwards over the stump, endangering anyone standing nearby. If we're lucky, some trees come down (not too near the house) during the frequent windstorms in winter. More often, we have to cut the trees ourselves, doing our best to use only those that are already dead or need to be thinned out.

Whichever way the trees end up on the ground, they all have a lot of branches. Many of the ones we cut are 80' tall or more, and it's not unusual for them to have branches 20' long and fairly heavy. For the past year or so, it's been my task to deal with the branches, which become my oven fuel. It's a lot of work. First I use the limbing axe to slice the branches away from the trunk of the tree. We cut mostly fir, so the next step is to cut off all the smaller branches that are mainly needles, leaving the woody parts. Then the stripped branches are cut to size, by

FIGURE 22.1. Rack built into the side of the oven shelter holds a good supply of oven fuel.

hand with a bow saw, and hauled to the oven shelter and stacked on the built-in wood rack to dry.

Pretty labor-intensive way of making oven fuel, sure. But I love it. First of all, no part of that tree is going to waste. (The green parts are composted.) Second, the smaller diameter of the branches means the wood burns faster and hotter than larger logs, because so much more surface area of the wood is exposed to the air. Third, if I wasn't cutting and hauling away the branches, they would pile up in the woods, eventually creating a fire hazard.

We do occasionally leave a few branches in strategic places in the woods as small-animal habitat. Many kinds of little birds nest close to the ground, and we've found they appreciate the protection from weather and predators afforded by a nice pile of evergreen branches. But generally, we prefer not to leave masses of branches to accumulate in the woods.

So most of my oven fuel is fir, a softwood like all conifers. We also cut Red Alder, a hardwood, and I add prunings from our apple trees, willows, and occasionally cottonwood to the mix.

Again, I'm no expert, but I do recommend using small-diameter wood like branches when you can. Of course, you can use other kinds of scrap wood; I occasionally have scraps of cedar fence boards or 2-by-4s that make good kindling. And when I hew cedar logs, as I did to make the framing for my oven shelter, the chunks of sapwood that are hewn away from the heartwood (called, mysteriously, "juggles") make wonderful kindling. We use these juggles for kindling in our woodstoves as well.

Peat as Oven Fuel

One of our two ponds is a natural peat bog. So far I haven't used peat for fuel in my oven, but someday I'm going to try it. As I wrote in *Craft Distilling*, Scotch whiskey gets its distinctive smoky taste from the barley that is dried over a peat fire after being malted. This began when the Scots were running out of wood to use as fuel and discovered that dried peat made a long-lasting, if smoky, fire. During World War II, in places where rationing meant shortages of fuel wood and coal along with food, desperation drove many people to try to stay warm by burning peat.

Peat, by the way, is not the same thing as peat moss. Peat, a precursor to coal, forms over hundreds of years as local vegetation falls to the ground and starts to decompose. As it accumulates, the weight of it gradually compresses the vegetation into a fairly solid mass that then resists decomposition because very little oxygen can penetrate it. The peat in our bog is quite solid and has to be laboriously dug out of the bank. Presumably it then has to be dried before burning.

How Much Wood Do You Need?

Well, that obviously depends on how large your oven is, how hot you want it to get, and how long you want it to stay hot enough to cook with. It also depends on how frequently you use your oven and how much thermal mass and insulation the oven has under the hearth and over the dome.

In general, heating my oven hot enough for pizza, followed by loaf bread and maybe some roasting meat, takes about a wheelbarrow of cut branches. Because of the large amount of thermal mass under the

FIGURE 22.2. This tree cut for firewood will yield several months' worth of oven fuel.

hearth, if I don't run the oven at least once a week, it can take several hours for the hearth to get hot enough to efficiently bake pizza and bread.

Starting the Fire

I never was a Girl Scout, although I was in Brownies for a while when I was young. I can remember my dad teaching us how to lay a fire in one of the several fireplaces in our house in Seattle when I was growing up, but I don't remember ever learning anything about combustion. The books I read before building the oven all mentioned combustion, and what else I know (so far) is a result of practice and experience.

Since we are using our woodstoves about eight months of the year, I've gotten in the habit of taking a scoop of hot coals from one of them to start my oven fire. I dump the coal on the hearth, toss on a few handfuls of cedar kindling, and give it some air with the bellows if needed. Usually it starts within seconds. Dry cedar is great for getting a fast, hot fire going, but it doesn't leave much, if any, coals, so I wouldn't use it for all my oven fuel; fir really is the best wood I have here for keeping a good hot fire going with lots of coals.

I discovered just recently that it's better to build a small fire, especially when I haven't fired up the oven for a while. I used to always get the fire going, then add wood frequently until it was getting pretty full of wood. I figured that I could then go away and leave it to burn without having to babysit it. I'm pretty sure that the reason it then took 4 or 5 hours to adequately heat up was because all that wood was blocking the air from flowing through the oven, increasing the combustion rate. Now I build a small fire, at least until I see that the hearth temperature is coming up nicely, and I find the oven is ready for baking in less than half the time it used to take.

Estimating Oven Temperature

Although I've been using this oven for about two years, I still am learning how to accurately gauge the right time to put in the food. One of these days, I will figure out a way to install a fourth thermocouple that will read the air temperature inside the oven, but even then, I suspect I will be on the learning curve a while yet.

I won't be able to tell you when your oven is ready for cooking or baking; there are too many variables involved. Smaller ovens will probably heat up faster than bigger ones; smaller pieces of fuel burn hotter and faster than large logs.

Coals in or out?

Should you leave the coals in the oven while you're cooking or baking, or rake them out? This kind of oven is sometimes called a "retained-heat" oven, which means just what it sounds like. The oven is heated with fire, then, when the optimum temperature is reached or nearly reached, the coals are raked out the oven door. The oven is then tightly closed up for an hour or more, allowing the temperature to equalize throughout the mass of the hearth and dome.

I hardly ever bother to rake out the coals before I cook. When baking four loaves of bread at a time, and not planning to cook anything else later, I do rake out the coals. My oven isn't all that big, but with pushing the bed of coals all the way to the back, it still leaves room for maybe three loaves in there at once. I do have to be careful baking bread with the coals still in the oven; they emit considerable radiant heat, and if I don't remember to let them die down fairly low first, I risk having the outside of my loaves get done or even burn before the inside is cooked.

I do like having that extra radiant heat when baking pizza, though. Flatbreads like pizza bake very well at high temperatures, and the extra bit of heat from the coals helps the cheese melt and the toppings and edge of the crust to brown nicely.

So Why Not Retire My Kitchen Oven?

If this oven is so great, why do I still use the gas oven in my kitchen? Simple. If I'm baking bread first thing in the morning, it just makes sense to do that indoors; I don't relish the idea of getting up at 2:00 a.m. to start the fire in the outdoor oven. In the winter, heating the gas oven is nice on those cold winter mornings, even with the woodstoves burning. And in the summer, having the option to use the wood-fired oven for baking bread is great.

The other obvious reason to use the gas oven is when I'm cooking or baking something that requires a more precise temperature. I'm pretty good at baking with the wood-fired oven, but I still can't actually control its temperature as accurately as I would like sometimes. If I'm baking cookies or something else that bakes fairly quickly, it doesn't make a lot of sense to spend a couple of hours heating up the outdoor oven.

As someone who loves to cook, I'm so thankful that I have the choice of these two ovens. Yes, I put a lot of effort into building the wood-fired oven, and I work hard at collecting fuel. But I love the results I get, and in a small way, it makes me feel a little more connected to the pioneers and homesteaders—including David's grandparents, who bought this property in the 1930s—whose lives revolved around this kind of hard work, figuring things out and doing it all by hand. There is something almost magical about the synergy of clay, water, grain, and fire in this process of baking bread in my wood-fired oven.

I hope I've inspired you to think about building your own oven, or collaborating with neighbors or friends to build one that the whole community can use and enjoy. I know many people who, with willing helpers pitching in, have built an oven, and started using it, in one weekend. It can be simple or elaborate, large or small, round or oval, brick or clay. Whatever your oven turns out to be, I can guarantee that the bread or pizza you make in it will be the best ever, because it is truly a labor of love.

Skillet Breads

*In the history of art
there are periods when bread seems so beautiful
that it nearly gets into museums.*
— JANET FLANNER

I'VE INCLUDED SEVERAL of my favorite bread recipes here, although scones and soda bread might not fit everyone's idea of bread, since they are traditionally leavened with baking powder and baking soda, respectively. Here's an idea: If you're cultivating a levain or barm starter, and find yourself with lots of extra starter, try stirring some into a batch of scones, soda bread, or some other quick bread, pancakes, or whatever. The slight acidity of the starter will react with the baking powder or soda, creating more CO_2 bubbles. It's up to you how much starter to add; use a smallish amount at first, until you get used to how it affects the baking. You might just come up with something totally unique and yummy! And you'll have the added satisfaction of not having wasted that starter.

Although these recipes include instructions for baking in your kitchen oven, all of them can be easily baked in your wood-fired oven.

Scones

I adore a good scone. I can't talk about scones, much less write about them, without baring my British roots for all and sundry to see, but that's just the way it is, love. Aside from a really good sourdough bread,

199

I can't think of anything I enjoy more than a warm scone, with currants and a little grated lemon peel mixed in, with real Devonshire cream and a nice hot cuppa. That's a real treat, though, one for a special occasion, and to be savored accordingly. Although I wouldn't mind if it got to be more of a regular thing.

 ## Lemon-currant Scones

Timing

- 5 to 10 minutes to measure ingredients and mix dough
- 30 minutes to shape and rest scones
- 20 minutes to bake

Equipment you'll definitely need

- Large mixing bowl (stainless steel, glass, Pyrex, or ceramic)
- Wooden spoon
- Sheet pan for baking
- Parchment paper
- Large cutting board

Stuff that's not absolutely necessary but recommended

- Kitchen scale
- Sifter
- Pastry cutter

Ingredients	Metric	US	Baker's %
• Unbleached all-purpose flour	350 g	2¾ cups	100
• Baking powder, aluminum-free	8 g	2 tsp	2.2
• Baking soda	1.5 g	¼ tsp	0.4
• Sea salt	5 g	¾ tsp	1.4
• Light brown sugar, packed	220 g	1 cup	63

• Currants	225 g	1½ cups	64
• Freshly grated lemon rind		2 to 3 tsp (2 lemons)	
• Unsalted butter, cold	340 g	1½ cups	97
• Buttermilk or light cream, cold	115 g	½ cup	33
• Egg, large, for egg wash	56 g	1	16
• Coarse sugar (optional)	about 40 g	3 Tbsp	11.4

Mixing the Dough

Stir or sift the flour, baking powder, baking soda, and salt into a large mixing bowl. Stir in the brown sugar, currants, and grated lemon peel.

Cut the cold butter into small pieces, and cut into the flour mixture, using a pastry cutter or your fingers. Work quickly, especially if using your fingers, to break up the butter into small pieces until the mixture has the consistency of coarse cornmeal. Add the buttermilk or cream, stirring just until the mixture comes together in a ball of dough; add a little more buttermilk or cream if needed.

Shaping and Resting the Scones

Cover your baking sheet with a piece of parchment paper. Turn out the dough on a lightly floured cutting board or clean counter surface. Use your hands to gently press the dough into a rough circle about 6" in diameter and about 1" thick. Cut the dough into 6 to 8 wedges and arrange them on the baking sheet. Cover the pan with plastic wrap, and refrigerate for at least 20 minutes while you preheat the oven.

Baking the Scones

Put one oven rack in the middle of the oven and preheat to 425°F (218°C). In a small bowl, beat the egg well and brush the beaten egg quickly over the tops of the scones. Dust the scones with coarse sugar if you like, then put the baking sheet in the oven.

Bake the scones for 10 minutes, then reduce the heat to 375°F (190°C). Turn the sheet pan around to help ensure even baking. Bake for another 10 minutes, or until the scones are golden brown. Cool on a rack for a few minutes before serving.

Irish Soda Bread

My mother's paternal great-grandmother, Bridget Stapleton, was Irish. Although she grew up in the Chicago area, it seems likely from ships' records that she was born on the voyage between Ireland and Boston in 1840. This was in the early days of the Irish Potato Famine, and many Irish were immigrating to the US or Canada at the time. Bridget's parents, William and Johanna Stapleton, were from County Tipperary, Ireland.

Mum used to make a lovely Irish stew, full of lamb and potatoes, and serve it with Irish soda bread. I remember being fascinated by the currants in the soda bread; for a long time, it was probably the only food I ever ate with currants in it. She baked it in two cake pans and cut it into thick wedges, to be eaten warm, slathered with butter (naturally). Here is her version, from the Redhed family recipe book. You'll notice the ingredients are very similar to scones, although this bread is only lightly sweetened.

Timing

- 5 to 10 minutes to measure ingredients and mix dough
- 5 minutes to divide and shape dough
- 35 to 40 minutes to bake

Equipment you'll definitely need

- Large mixing bowl (stainless steel, glass, Pyrex, or ceramic)
- Wooden spoon
- Two 8″ cake or pie pans
- Sharp knife for dividing and scoring dough
- Large cutting board

Stuff that's not absolutely necessary but recommended

- Kitchen scale
- Pastry cutter

Ingredients	Metric	US	Baker's %
• Unbleached all-purpose flour	500 g	about 4 cups	100
• Baking powder, aluminum-free	12 g	1 Tbsp	2.4
• Baking soda	6 g	1 tsp	1.2
• Sea salt	7 g	1 tsp	1.4
• Granulated sugar	50 g	¼ cup	10
• Ground cardamom or coriander (optional)		⅛ tsp	
• Unsalted butter, cold, cut in small pieces	57 g	¼ cup	11
• Raisins or currants	300 g	2 cups	60
• Egg, large	56 g	1	11
• Buttermilk or light cream, cold	400 g	1¾ cups	80

Mixing the Dough

Stir or sift the flour, baking powder and soda, salt, sugar, and carda-mom or coriander into a large mixing bowl. Add the butter, cutting it in with a pastry blender or your fingers until the mixture is crumbly and the butter is dispersed throughout.

In a small bowl, beat the egg slightly and whisk in the buttermilk or cream. Stir this mixture into the flour mixture until blended. Turn the dough out onto a lightly floured cutting board, and knead for about 2 or 3 minutes, just until the dough is smooth.

Shaping and Baking the Soda Bread

Preheat your oven to 375°F (190°C). Divide the dough in half with a sharp knife. Shape each piece into a rounded loaf. Put each loaf into an 8" cake or pie pan, pressing dough gently with your fingers to fill the pan. Using a sharp knife, make two cuts across the tops of the loaves in a cross shape, about ½" deep at the top. Bake for 35 to 40 minutes. Cool briefly on cooling racks, then remove the soda bread from the pans. Serve warm or at room temperature.

Focaccia

Focaccia is a simple flatbread that, like pizza, varies in its ingredients and toppings from one region to another in Italy. According to Carol Field, author of *The Italian Baker* (see Appendix B), as the Roman Empire extended through western Europe, they brought their traditional flatbreads with them. The hearth breads of England and the French *fougasse*, then, share a common ancestry with the Italian focaccia.

Traditional focaccia is either a large round or rectangle and can be thick or thin, soft or crisp, and have very few or more elaborate toppings. The local olive oil, olives, and herbs can be stirred into the dough or simply scattered on the top just before baking. This is one of the things I love most about simple, rustic breads like focaccia; once the dough is made and in the pan, you can top it with just about anything that is on hand or in season. It will be a little different each time but always delicious and so easy to make. It is the perfect thing for snacking or taking on picnics. Or make a simple meal of focaccia along with a seasonal salad and roast chicken…my favorite!

Although this bread is baked in a pan, you can set the pan on a preheated baking stone if you wish.

Timing

- 10 to 15 minutes to measure ingredients and mix dough
- 1½ hours to ferment dough
- 40 minutes to shape and rest focaccia

Equipment you'll definitely need

- Large mixing bowl (stainless steel, glass, Pyrex, or ceramic)
- Wooden spoon and wire whisk
- Large cutting board
- Jelly roll pan or other baking sheet about 10½" × 15½"

Stuff that's not absolutely necessary but recommended

- Kitchen scale
- 2-quart dough-rising bucket with lid
- Pastry brush
- Baking stone

Ingredients	Metric	US	Baker's %
• SAF or other instant yeast	4 g	1 tsp	0.8
• Unchlorinated water, warm	60 g	¼ cup	12
• Unchlorinated water, room temperature	236 g	1 cup	47
• Extra-virgin olive oil	30 g	2 Tbsp	6
• Unbleached bread flour	500 g	3¾ cups	100
• Sea salt	10 g	1½ tsp	2

Mixing and Kneading the Dough

In a large mixing bowl, stir the yeast into the warm water. Stir in the rest of the water and the olive oil. Add about half the flour and the salt, and mix with a wooden spoon or whisk until batter is smooth. Gradually stir in the rest of the flour, continuing to stir until the dough comes together. Knead the dough for about 10 minutes, taking a break in the middle for a few minutes if you want to. As with most breads, I like to dip my hand in cool water while kneading, rather than flouring my hands, to keep the dough moist and less dense. But if you find it easier to knead dough on a floured board, that's fine too.

Fermenting the Dough

Put the dough in your dough-rising bucket and put the lid on, or just cover the dough in the mixing bowl with plastic wrap. Let it ferment at room temperature until the dough has doubled in volume; if you're using the dough-rising bucket, the dough will fill the bucket when it has doubled.

Shaping and Resting the Dough

Lightly oil the jelly roll pan with olive oil. Turn the dough out on a lightly floured board. Using your hands, press the dough into a rough rectangle, then roll it out to fit in the jelly roll pan. Place in the pan, cover with plastic wrap or a clean kitchen towel, and let rest for 30 minutes.

Dimpling and Fermenting the Dough

Using your fingertips, dimple the entire surface of the dough; don't be afraid to be enthusiastic! These little dimples will hold delicious little pools of olive oil and sea salt. Cover the dimpled dough, and let ferment again for about 2 hours; it should double in bulk and fairly well fill up the pan.

While the dough is fermenting, line up your toppings. You can simply use olive oil and sea salt, or go on to add chopped fresh herbs, olives, cheeses, or whatever you have on hand that looks good at the time. I love using fresh rosemary on focaccia; sadly, it is too cold in winter where I live to successfully grow rosemary myself, but I have generous friends nearby who share their herbs with me.

Adding Toppings and Baking the Focaccia

Preheat your oven to 400°F (204°C). If you're using a baking stone, put it on a middle rack, and start preheating the oven at least 30 minutes before baking. Using a pastry brush or your fingers, spread a generous amount of extra-virgin olive oil over the top of the focaccia. Sprinkle with sea salt, then put on your additional toppings.

Put the pan directly onto a baking stone or onto the oven rack, and bake for 20 to 25 minutes. The focaccia will puff up a bit and look golden brown. When the focaccia is finished baking, take it out of the pan right away so the bottom of the bread doesn't get soggy. Enjoy your focaccia while it is still warm or at room temperature. It is best eaten when fresh; don't succumb to the temptation to put it in the refrigerator. If we have any left over the day after baking, David likes to reheat it on a cast-iron griddle on our gas stove or the wood-fired cookstove.

Chapattis

This past year or so, I have been slowly learning a bit about Indian cooking. David has a wonderful Indian cookbook, another of those Time-Life books, called simply *The Cooking of India*. It was published in the late 1960s, and some of the ingredients and equipment called for reflect the times. Chickens, for instance. When I was learning to make tandoori chicken, I looked it up in that book. The method called for chickens 2 to 3 pounds in size! The standard supermarket chicken these days, the Cornish Cross hybrid, is easily twice that size.

Anyway, I had fun looking through that book and learning about Indian breads and getting pleasantly sidetracked on Indian feast day celebrations and recipes for various masalas. I had no idea there were so many different kinds of bread in India, but then I had no idea they even grew wheat there (blush). In northern India, chapattis are a well-known unleavened whole-wheat flatbread, easily and quickly made in a large skillet or on the hearth of your wood-fired oven.

Timing

- 7 to 10 minutes to measure ingredients and mix dough
- 1 hour to ferment dough
- 5 to 10 minutes to divide and shape dough
- 10 to 20 minutes to bake chapattis

Equipment you'll definitely need

- Large mixing bowl (stainless steel, glass, Pyrex, or ceramic)
- Wooden spoon
- Sharp knife for dividing dough
- Large cutting board
- Large (10″ to 12″ diameter) cast-iron skillet
- Large spatula
- Rolling pin

Stuff that's not absolutely necessary but recommended

• Kitchen scale

Ingredients	Metric	US	Baker's %
• Stone-ground whole wheat flour	400 g	3½ cups	100
• Sea salt	7 g	1¼ tsp	1.7
• Unchlorinated water, cool	295 g	1¼ cups	73

Mixing and Kneading the Dough

Combine whole wheat flour, salt, and water in a mixing bowl, stirring to form a dough. Turn out onto a lightly floured board, and knead dough for about 5 minutes; the dough should be smooth and not sticky.

Fermenting the Dough

Put the dough back in the mixing bowl, and cover with plastic wrap. Refrigerate the dough for 1 hour.

Shaping and Cooking the Chapattis

Take the dough out of the refrigerator. On a lightly floured cutting board, cut the dough into pieces, about 7 to 14, depending on the size of your skillet. Roll out each piece, forming a circle about ⅛" thick.

Heat a cast-iron skillet (10" to 12" diameter) over medium-high heat. Lightly oil the pan with canola or peanut oil (or lightly mist with cooking spray if you prefer). Use the spatula to put a chapatti in the pan. Cook for 10 seconds, then flip it over, and cook for about 1 minute; the chapatti will develop brown spots as the starches gelatinize. Flip it over again, and cook until the chapatti starts to balloon in the middle. Use a potholder to lightly press down on the dough to flatten it. Remove from the pan when the bottom has browned lightly.

Put the cooked chapatti on a clean kitchen towel, and continue cooking the rest of the chapattis. You can stack the chapattis to keep them warm, wrapping them in the towel as you go.

But Wait, There's More!

By now you might be getting the idea of how easy it is to substitute gluten-free grains for the wheat flour in all the recipes in this chapter. Flatbreads in general, because by definition they don't rise very much during baking (particularly unleavened ones like chapattis), can lend themselves very well to gluten-free versions. With all the choices in grains, and gluten-free grains becoming more easily available these days, there are almost endless ways to tweak recipes to suit your needs and taste. The next chapter offers two more of my favorite flatbread recipes, ones I particularly like to bake in the wood-fired oven when I have the chance.

Freshly baked wood-fired sourdough loaf.

Seeded sourdough bread, sliced.

Baked
sourdough
loaf.

Three loaves
of sourdough
bread, just
put in the
wood-fired
oven.

Seeded
sourdough loaf.

Baked
whole-wheat
miche
showing
score marks.

Whole-wheat
miche,
a classic
French
whole-grain
bread.

Dough after kneading.

Fermented dough, just before shaping.

Bread dough at start of fermentation.

Dough after shaping.

Freshly baked,
aromatic rye bread.

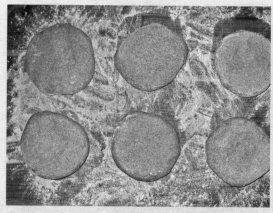

English muffins, shaped and proofing.

English muffins baking on a cast-iron griddle.

Pita bread (*left*), and bialys (*right*), baked in the wood-fired oven.

Bialys ready to bake.

Neapolitan-style pizza.

Unbaked Pizza alla Marinara.

Wood-fired Pizza alla Marinara.

Wood-fired Pizza Margherita.

Baked
Montreal-
style bagels
on cooling
rack.

Mum's
coffeecake,
iced, warm,
and ready
to eat.

Naan and Pita:
Two Favorite Flatbreads

TWO OF MY FAVORITE flatbreads are the Indian *naan*, and the pocket bread called *pita*. Many countries have versions of pocket bread, but the one most familiar to Americans is the Greek pita. Both these breads are perfect for baking on the hearth in your wood-fired oven; indeed, in India naan is traditionally baked by slapping the dough on the inside of the walls of a clay tandoori oven. Pita needs high baking heat to produce the large air pocket as the gas expands, so the intense heat of the wood-fired oven is ideal. Indian cooks believe that the clay of the oven itself contributes to the flavor of anything cooked in the tandoori oven, and I can testify from experience that things like marinated chickens and roasted vegetables taste positively amazing when cooked in my wood-fired oven.

Still, you can make wonderful naan, pita, and other flatbreads in your kitchen oven, especially if you have a baking stone. The naan recipe calls for both yeast and a generous amount of poolish or other sponge starter (see Chapter 12). The basic recipe calls for unbleached bread flour, but you can substitute whole wheat flour for part of the bread flour; I would use maybe ⅓ to ½ whole wheat flour. Using ghee (recipe p. 214) to moisten your hands before shaping the naan is optional, but I highly recommend it; it lends another layer of incomparable taste to the finished naan.

Naan

Timing

- 15 to 20 minutes to mix and knead dough
- 1 hour to ferment dough
- 1¼ hours to divide, preshape and refrigerate dough
- 15 to 20 minutes to shape naan
- 3 to 5 minutes to bake naan

Equipment you'll definitely need

- Large mixing bowl (stainless steel, glass, Pyrex, or ceramic)
- Wooden spoon
- Large cutting board
- Sharp knife for dividing dough
- Large baking sheet
- Parchment paper

Stuff that's not absolutely necessary but recommended

- Kitchen scale
- 2-quart dough-rising bucket
- Baking stone
- Clean kitchen towel

Ingredients	Metric	US	Baker's %
• Unbleached bread flour	500 g	about 3⅔ cups	100
• Sea salt	13 g	2 tsp	2.6
• SAF or other instant yeast	3 g	1 tsp	0.6
• Extra-virgin olive oil	55 g	4 Tbsp	11
• Plain yogurt	125 g	½ cup	25
• Poolish or other sponge starter	500 g	about 2 cups	100
• Unchlorinated water, cool, as needed			
• Ghee (see recipe p. 214)	45 to 60 g	3 to 4 Tbsp	

Mixing and Kneading the Dough

In a large mixing bowl, combine the flour, salt, yeast, olive oil, yogurt and poolish, stirring to blend thoroughly, and form a ball of dough. Knead the dough for a total of 12 to 15 minutes, dipping your hands in cool water as needed to keep the dough from sticking. It's perfectly fine to divide the time in half, taking a break for about 10 minutes before finishing the kneading. In fact, this is my usual routine; the brief rest is good for both me and my dough.

Fermenting the Dough

Put the dough into your dough-rising bucket if you have one, and put on the lid. Or just leave it in the mixing bowl, and cover it with plastic wrap. Let the dough ferment for an hour at room temperature. It will expand noticeably, although it may not double in volume.

Dividing and Preshaping the Dough

Turn the dough out onto a lightly floured board. Using a sharp knife, divide the dough into 6 to 8 pieces. Form each piece into a rough round. Line a baking sheet with parchment paper and dust the paper lightly with flour. Put the dough pieces on the parchment paper, cover loosely with plastic wrap, and refrigerate for an hour.

Shaping and Baking the Naan

Preheat your oven to 550°F (287°C) or the hottest temperature you can, placing your baking stone (if you're using one) on a middle rack. It will take a good hour to thoroughly preheat that baking stone, so you might want to start preheating it about half an hour before you take the dough out of the fridge.

Moisten your hands with a little ghee and pick up a ball of dough, flattening it gently into a disk. Holding the dough by one edge, let it hang, gently shaking it a bit to encourage it to stretch without pulling it too much. Turn the dough so you're holding it by another edge; repeat 2 or 3 times, until the dough has stretched to a rough rectangle or oval shape and is about ½" thick.

TIP

You're shaping this thing by hand, not rolling it out with a rolling pin, so don't expect the thickness to be consistent. Just aim for most of the piece to be about ½" thick. If you're substituting whole wheat flour for part of the bread flour, you may not be able to get it that thin without the dough tearing. That's perfectly okay. I want you to enjoy this process, not be so stressed out that you swear off making naan ever again.

You can start baking your naan as soon as you have shaped one or two pieces, but since it bakes pretty quickly at this temperature, I think it's easier to do all the shaping first and then bake. You'll need to have several pieces of parchment paper on the counter, on baking sheets, or a nearby table.

When you're ready, you can either drop the naan directly onto the hot baking stone or use a peel to transfer the naan, parchment paper and all, onto the stone. You can probably guess which method I prefer. My baking stone handles two of these breads at once, so I like to put two of them on parchment paper and slide them onto the stone with my peel.

Bake the naan for 3 to 5 minutes. It will look puffy, and you'll see brown spots forming as it bakes. Use a peel or large spatula to take the naans out of the oven. You can keep the naan warm by wrapping them in a clean kitchen towel.

Naan is best eaten fresh, either warm or at room temperature. A traditional Indian meal, popular all over the country, is roasted tandoori chicken, fresh naan, and *salat*, a simple vegetable salad. Just incredible!

Ghee

Okay, first of all, ghee is actually not the same thing as clarified butter. To make clarified butter, you pretty much just melt the butter and skim the foam off the top. Ghee is melted, then cooked at low heat for 45 minutes, during which time the milk solids caramelize, forming brown crusty bits at the bottom of the pan. It is then easy to pour off the perfectly clear ghee.

I've been making ghee for my mother, who is lactose-intolerant, for quite a while now, and I am totally sold on its benefits. For one thing, and this is particularly meaningful for me and others who live off the grid or who want to be prepared with extra food in case of emergencies, unlike fresh butter, ghee keeps for months and months at room temperature. I love having at least a couple of pint jars of ghee on my pantry shelf. Ghee also has a much higher smoke point than plain butter (and many cooking oils), so it is ideal as a cooking fat where the buttery flavor is an asset. And because the process of making ghee cooks out the milk solids and water, leaving pure butterfat, Mum can enjoy the incomparable flavor of butter with no worries.

Maybe this is just me, but since I often eat ghee on toast and other things at Mum's place, I honestly think it has an even more buttery taste than plain old butter. I know that sounds odd, but I love the taste of ghee. Try it yourself, I'll bet you end up agreeing.

I prefer to use unsalted butter to make ghee. The flavor of the butter gets a bit concentrated as it cooks, and I just like to decide for myself how much salt to add when I'm using ghee.

Ghee is very easy to make. One pound (454 g) of butter makes one pint of ghee, or a little less. You'll need a saucepan with a fairly heavy bottom; you don't need a lid.

Put 454 g (1 pound/4 sticks/2 cups) of unsalted butter in your saucepan, and melt over medium heat. Once melted, the surface of the butter will be covered with foam. Increase the heat, and bring the butter to a boil.

Important: Do *not* put the lid on the pan at any point while making ghee. Condensation forms on the inside of the lid, and you don't want that dripping into the butter.

When it is bubbly all over, immediately turn the heat down. On my gas stove, I turn the flame down as low as it can go. When I made ghee recently on my mother's glass-cooktop electric stove, it took a little tweaking to find the right setting. *Do not stir* once you turn the heat down. You want the butter to be lightly bubbling throughout the cooking time, in order to completely separate out the milk solids. Very soon the butter should begin to look clear; if it still looks milky or opaque, turn the heat up a little bit.

Cook, uncovered, without stirring, for 45 minutes. Remove from the heat, and strain slowly and carefully; I like to use several layers of good-quality cheesecloth inside a strainer placed over a large mixing bowl. Try not to disturb the solids at the bottom of the pan any more than necessary while straining.

If something doesn't taste right, just add a little butter!
— Julia Child

Pour the strained ghee into clean Mason jars; I like wide-mouth pint jars for this. It should look beautifully clear and golden brown. As it cools it will become fairly solid. As I've said, properly made ghee will last for months at room temperature. Some methods say to process it in a boiling-water bath, but for fairly short-term storage that really isn't necessary, and I'm not sure what the advantage of processing is. I like to have a couple of jars on the shelf, but we use it up quite promptly, so long-term storage issues have never arisen.

Pita (Pocket Bread)

Timing

- 15 to 20 minutes to mix and knead dough
- 90 minutes to ferment dough
- 20 to 30 minutes to divide, preshape, and rest dough
- 3 minutes to bake

Equipment you'll definitely need

- Large mixing bowl (stainless steel, glass, Pyrex, or ceramic)
- Wooden spoon
- Sharp knife for dividing dough
- Rolling pin
- Long-handled tongs or large spatula

Stuff that's not absolutely necessary but recommended

- Kitchen scale
- 2-quart dough-rising bucket
- Parchment paper
- Baking stone
- Pizza peel or rimless baking sheet

Ingredients	Metric	US	Baker's %
• Unbleached bread flour	500 g	about 3⅔ cups	100
• Sea salt	10 g	1 tsp	2
• SAF or other instant yeast	6 g	2 tsp	1.2
• Extra-virgin olive oil	30 g	2 Tbsp	6
• Unchlorinated water, cool	300 g	1¼ cups	60

Mixing and Kneading the Dough

Combine all ingredients in a large mixing bowl, stirring to form a ball of dough. Knead the dough for a total of 12 to 15 minutes, dipping your hands in cool water as needed to keep the dough from sticking. Take a 10-minute break in the middle of kneading if you want. The dough will be fairly soft and springy.

Fermenting the Dough

Put the dough into your dough-rising bucket if you have one, and put on the lid. Or just leave it in the mixing bowl and cover it with plastic wrap. Let the dough ferment for 90 minutes at room temperature.

FIGURE 24.1. Pita bread (*left*) baked in the wood-fired oven; baked bialys (Chapter 9) are on the right.

It should double in volume; if you're using a dough-rising bucket the bucket will fill up when the dough doubles.

Dividing and Preshaping the Pita

Line a baking sheet with parchment paper, and dust the paper lightly with flour. Turn the dough out onto a lightly floured board. Using a sharp knife, divide the dough into 4 to 8 pieces. Round each piece, then flatten them into disks. Lay the disks on the parchment paper, cover loosely with plastic wrap, and let the dough rest for 20 minutes.

Shaping and Baking the Pita

Preheat your oven to 475°F (246°C), with your baking stone (if you're using one) on a bottom rack. Be sure to allow at least 45 minutes to properly preheat the baking stone.

On a floured board, roll out each disk about ¼" thick. If you have 4 pieces, the pitas will be close to 12" in diameter; if you have 8 pieces, they will be closer to 6" in diameter. I like to have several sheets of parchment paper, sized to fit my baking stone, lined up: one on my peel and a couple more on the counter. After the pitas are rolled out, lay them on the parchment paper, and let them rest for 10 minutes.

You can bake as many pitas at one time as will fit on your baking stone or baking sheet, but I prefer to do two at a time. These things bake so quickly, I like to be able to get them in and out of the oven efficiently, and when I'm working by myself, two at a time is enough for me.

Slide the pitas, parchment paper and all, onto the hot baking stone and bake for about 3 minutes. They will balloon as the moisture in the dough turns to steam in the high heat. Take them out as soon as they have ballooned; you don't want these breads to bake until they are browned, they will be too crisp once they cool.

Transfer the pitas to a cooling rack. A long-handled pair of tongs is useful for picking up and moving them; it doesn't matter if you deflate the pitas in the process, they do that on their own while they cool anyway.

TIP

At this point, you can also put the baking sheet in the refrigerator and chill the dough for up to 2 days.

TIP

If your pita doesn't puff up as it should (there always seems to be one in every crowd, right?), just use it as you would any other flatbread. Put a few toppings on it, pop it back into the oven for a few minutes, and hey presto! Mini pizza! Or just fold it over and make your half-moon sandwich that way.

Go to Your Kitchen and Play!

There comes a point in your life
when you need to stop eating other people's bread
and make your own.
— CHRIS GEIGER

I HOPE THAT BY NOW you're having fun baking bread, whatever your comfort zone. I truly believe there is something in this book for just about anyone who really wants to learn to make bread. Guess what? This is just the beginning! Once you find your comfort zone and make handmade bread a part of your life, who knows what else you will discover inside yourself? No-knead bread, long-fermented sourdough, or something in between, it doesn't matter. I know for a fact that you will enjoy, just as much as I do, baking your own bread and hearing your own friends and family say, "Wow, something sure smells great in here!"

If you have worked your way through most or all of this book, you will no doubt have picked up the idea that bread is really very simple. It's flour, salt, yeast, and water. I have deliberately kept the number of recipes included here to a minimum because I want you to get comfortable with the basic processes, not overwhelm you to the point of mind-numbing tedium. If you're feeling frisky and ready to stretch yourself a bit, take those basic formulas and methods and tweak them!

Swap out some of the bread flour for a gluten-free flour; think outside the loaf pan and have fun shaping a free-form loaf; slash your initials on your sourdough bread if you want to. It's your bread, so game on, my friend!

Adapting Recipes

By using the basic formula in Chapter 8, you can easily adapt recipes, whether to fit your dietary needs and your preferences, or your schedule, or even just for the fun of it. For example:

* If you want to lower your gluten intake but love your bread as much as I do, try substituting part of the total flour in the recipe with the Gluten-free Baking Mix in Chapter 18.
* Say you planned to make sourdough bread, something came up and you don't have time for a 24-hour process; try making a biga instead of refreshing your sourdough starter as usual.
* Or, if you're already started your dough and need to slow down the process for whatever reason, just put your dough in a dough bucket in the fridge until you're ready to get back to it.
* Any recipe calling for a pre-ferment like biga or poolish can be adapted for long fermentation by simply substituting levain or another storage leaven for the pre-ferment. And the reverse is also true, of course; you can swap your recipe's storage leaven for a pre-ferment and speed up the process a bit.
* Your ideas here

You'll undoubtedly think of many variations and improvisations that haven't occurred to me. This is one of the many things I love about cooking in general: Once you get comfortable with the basics and have enough experience to have some confidence, experimenting is a lot of fun. There are so many different flours to try, different leavening methods, even different types of ovens. And, you'll learn new skills that you will be proud to pass on to your children.

In Defense of Bread

So, is bread actually good for you? Given the combination of whole grains (for fiber) and long fermentation, the answer is **yes**. Fiber helps control the release of glucose into the bloodstream, minimizing spikes in the blood sugar. Fiber also promotes good intestinal health and regularity. Long fermentation of bread dough helps neutralize gluten, making it more digestible for people with gluten sensitivities; it also improves the flavor and shelf life of sourdough breads.

Wheat and other grains have been nourishing humans for thousands of years. Something like 40% of the worldwide population relies on wheat for much of its daily nutrition. However, if you believe, or suspect, that you may be sensitive to gluten or something else in wheat, please talk to your nutritionist or naturopath; don't just rely on scaremongering books or blogs. Until we have a testing methodology for accurately diagnosing non-celiac gluten sensitivity (NCGS), you really need to take charge of your own health. Get the facts, as best you can.

Once again, it is a quality-of-life issue. I can tell you, from years of experience, that one of the best ways to get more in tune with your body, your health, and nutrition is to make at least some of your own food. Why not start with bread?

There are all sorts of metaphors about bread and its importance in our lives. I'm convinced that the actual process of making bread— of mixing flour, salt, yeast, and water to create sustenance for our bodies—has some kind of deeper spiritual meaning in the big picture of our lives.

We've come a long way from Wonder bread, haven't we?

Afterword

Gosh. It seems every writing project brings with it new layers of surprise. Six years ago, I would never have believed I would be a published author; I didn't even know I was a writer. And this, my third book...a cookbook? Really? I suppose in a way it shouldn't be so surprising; thanks to my mother and a lot of trial, error, and practice, making bread has been a part of my life for more than 40 years.

Although the work of the author is naturally the most visible part of a book, many other people are involved in the process of bringing a book to publication. Of these, there are a few people I must mention by name; there is a point where it's not enough to say simply, "You know who you are." To those whose names are not included here, I can assure you that your contributions to the research, publication, and ultimate success of this book are much appreciated.

To Publishing Director Sue Custance, Managing Editor Ingrid Witvoet, and all the other terrific people at New Society Publishers, without whom this book might never have progressed beyond my flour-dusted kitchen, I am so grateful for your support and expertise.

To my fantastically patient and skilled copy-editor, Judith Brand, who has helped make all three of my books fit for publication: with your help and encouragement, I am slowly but surely improving as a writer. I'm so grateful for your attention to detail, and your amazing ability to fix, change, and tweak things while preserving my voice and style.

To Andrew Perkins and Robert Riley, the amazing young leaders of the Mother Earth News Fair crew, thanks ever so much for continuing to invite me to speak about bread at the Fairs and promote my books. Like my publisher, you gave a complete beginner an opportunity that has literally changed my life.

And to my husband David, who manfully taste-tested his way through loaf after loaf, and who goaded me—oops, I mean encouraged me—to take on the task of building a wood-fired oven.

There are also many who, although I do not know your names, have been instrumental in the creation of this book and its progress from nebulous concept to finished product. You were in the audience at my presentations, book signings, and demonstrations in several cities across the country, between October 2016 and the day this book went to press. You came in large numbers; you asked really great questions, and were so eager to learn! You might not have known it, but you helped me realize that I needed to revise my initial plan for this book, which was intended to focus on sourdough breads. Truly, my main object all along was to encourage you to simply *make bread*, in whatever way was most comfortable for you. I listened to your questions, shifted gears, and I believe this book is much better as a result.

My heartfelt thanks to each and every one of you. I am so very grateful for yet another opportunity to share what I have learned with each one of you. That's *my* comfort zone.

Appendix A:
Converting Weights and Measures

As you know, I recommend measuring ingredients by weight rather than by volume. It is not only more accurate (especially for liquids), I think it is also easier. Yes, you'll need to get a decent kitchen scale that measures in grams as well as ounces, but it's not a major investment these days. And it will come in handy for other things too; you might not send things by post as often as I do, but when you're wondering if that fancy musical greeting card is going to need an extra stamp, it sure is nice to have that scale!

I've used a lot of different flours over the years, and it somehow still surprises me that not all flours weigh the same for a given volume. In the table below, I've included just a few of the flours most commonly used in baking, as well as several other ingredients you'll find in recipes in this book. This chart shows US amounts converted to grams.

Ingredient	¼ cup	½ cup	¾ cup	1 cup	2 cups
Bread flour	34 g	68 g	102 g	136 g	272 g
All-purpose flour	32 g	64 g	96 g	128 g	256 g
Whole wheat flour	28 g	56 g	85 g	113 g	226 g
Granulated sugar	50 g	100 g	150 g	200 g	400 g
Brown sugar, packed	55 g	110 g	165 g	220 g	440 g
Powdered sugar	32 g	64 g	96 g	128 g	256 g
Butter	57 g	113 g	171 g	227 g	454 g
Milk	57 g	114 g	173 g	230 g	460 g
Water	59 g	118 g	177 g	236 g	472 g

A chart of egg sizes and weights isn't often included in this kind of appendix, but since I advocate weighing ingredients, I'm including eggs.

We've raised poultry since 2007, and I promise you, chicken eggs vary a lot in size. So sometimes it's handy to be able to weigh them, if a recipe calls for large or extra-large eggs and you're not sure what you have.

Egg type	Small	Medium	Large	Extra large	Jumbo
Chicken	42–49 g (1½–1¾ oz.)	49–56 g (1¾–2 oz.)	56–63 g (2–2¼ oz.)	63–70 g (2¼–2½ oz.)	Over 70 g (over 2½ oz.)
Duck					84 g or more (3+ oz.)

Temperature Conversions

To convert Fahrenheit temperatures to Celsius, subtract 32, multiply the result by 5, then divide that number by 9. Example:

212°F: 212−32=180; 180×5=900; 900÷9=100; So, 212°F = 100°C

To convert Celsius temperatures to Fahrenheit, reverse the calculation: Multiply the number by 9, divide by 5 and add 32. Example:

246°C: 246×9=2214; 2214÷5=443 (442.8); 443+32=475; So 246°C=475°F.

Here are some temperatures commonly used in cooking and baking, in Fahrenheit and Celsius.

	Degrees Fahrenheit	Degrees Celsius
Water, simmering	115	46
Water, scalding	130	54
Water, boiling (sea level)	212	100
Very low oven	250 to 275	121 to 133
Low oven	300 to 325	149 to 163
Moderate oven	350 to 375	177 to 190
Hot oven	400 to 425	204 to 218
Very hot oven	450 to 475	232 to 246
Really damned hot	500 to 525	260 to 274

Appendix B:
Recommended Books and
Other Resources

I own, and use, every one of these books. There's something for everyone here, so when you feel ready, you'll find an amazing world of bread you can make at home, regardless of your comfort zone.

Artisan Bread in 5 Minutes a Day
by Jeff Hertzberg and Zoë François
I've included this book mainly because it has a lot of good recipes using the no-knead technique. I have a bit of a quibble, though, with the emphasis on 5 minutes a day. Anyone who decides to try to bake bread probably assumes it's going to take some time and allows for that. Also, some of the recipes definitely take more than 5 minutes.

The Bread Builders: Hearth Loaves and Masonry Ovens
by Daniel Wing and Alan Scott
Many people consider this book the bible of artisan bread-making. Along with in-depth discussion of the scientific basis of bread production, it has instructions for building a professional-size, brick wood-fired oven. It was published in 1999 and includes a profile of the well-known champion of the artisan bread world, Chad Robertson, when he was still in his twenties. Not a recipe book in the usual sense, it focuses more on the techniques and skills of bread-making plus profiles of some of the better-known artisan bakeries in America.

Build Your Own Earth Oven
by Kiko Denzer and Hannah Field
This is a little book packed with very useful information. It not only covers in detail the whole process of building your own wood-fired clay oven by

hand, it also has a section on making sourdough bread. If you want to build a bread oven, one that can be made with easily available and affordable materials, I highly recommend this book. Most of the work I did building my oven was based on the advice and ideas presented here, and it's inspiring to see photos of very beautiful and imaginative ovens that others have built. One caution: The bread-making part was written by a co-author who was formerly a professional baker. I agree with her advice to not stress out about baking bread, but I don't think it's very easy for beginners to understand without clearly defined parameters in recipes and techniques. For more experienced bakers, though, I do like her approach to sourdough bread.

Crust and Crumb: Master Formulas for Serious Bread Bakers
by Peter Reinhart
Once you've found your comfort zone with bread-making, I definitely recommend this book. Peter Reinhart is arguably the best-known bread writer in America, and here he presents an impressive lineup of master recipes and techniques for making all kinds of breads.

Flatbreads and Flavors: A Baker's Atlas
by Jeffrey Alford and Naomi Duguid
Winner of the James Beard Award for cookbooks, this book is packed with recipes from around the world, collected during the extensive travels of the bread-loving authors. It not only offers wonderful recipes for flatbreads, organized by country, it also includes recipes for soups, salsas, and other foods traditionally eaten with those breads. I highly recommend this book for anyone either lowering or eliminating their gluten intake. Although flatbreads are obviously not the same as the sandwich breads we're used to, they offer a lot of choices for making breads not so dependent on the rising power of gluten.

Grain of Truth: The Real Case for and Against Wheat and Gluten
by Stephen Yafa
The author of *Grain of Truth* is a journalist who got curious about gluten when his wife was told at an Ayurvedic retreat that she must avoid gluten. For over a year, he traveled, researched, and learned about wheat and gluten. As the subtitle says, the book gives a balanced look at both sides of the issue of whether wheat and gluten are good for humans or are foods we should avoid at all costs because of their health risks. If you've been wondering if there's something to all the scary information out there about

gluten or if it's all a lot of undeserved hype, do read this book before you make up your mind.

The Italian Baker
by Carol Field
This updated version of Carol Field's wonderful tour of Italian baking is an excellent book for anyone wanting to delve more deeply into Italy's repertoire of fabulous breads, pizzas, pastries, cookies, and cakes. It offers very good information about basic techniques and ingredients, and bread recipes include instructions for mixing by machine as well as by hand.

The Laurel's Kitchen Bread Book: A Guide to Whole-Grain Breadmaking
by Laurel Robertson
The updated version of this classic book includes detailed information on making bread using a bread machine. Excellent book for anyone wanting specifically to make whole-grain breads. Also has detailed instructions for creating and maintaining a desem starter, so if you're interested in desem bread, this book is well worth purchasing for that alone.

Local Breads: Sourdough and Whole-grain Recipes
from Europe's Best Artisan Bakers
by Daniel Leader
This is one of my favorite bread books ever, although I recommend it mainly for bread bakers with a little bit of experience who want to explore the world of sourdough more deeply. "Local breads" refers to the indigenous wild yeasts that vary from region to region, allowing bakers to make truly local sourdough that can't be duplicated elsewhere. Dan Leader, who owns the well-known Daily Bread bakery in upstate New York, traveled through several European countries, working with some of the best local bakers to learn new techniques and recipes. He's adapted these recipes for American kitchens and ingredients and includes useful FAQs in each section. I particularly love the stories of his experiences as he traveled, learned, and baked his way through European bakeries.

On Food and Cooking
by Harold McGee
Food geeks rejoice: Harold McGee's ambitious yet highly readable book explains everything you always wanted to know about the science behind food and cooking. It covers much more than grains, flours, and baking

techniques, but if you just read those parts, you'll add greatly to your understanding of the baking process and why things happen the way they do. I highly recommend this excellent resource.

Websites

I'm always a little hesitant to list websites, given how frequently they come and go and how infrequently some of them are updated or maintained. Plus, websites aren't usually the first resource I head for, being off the grid without high-speed Internet at home; I have books and magazines for that, until I get out to the coffee shop.

Your Google search is as good as mine, but if you're interested in more whole-grain baking, do spend some time looking around the Whole Grain Connection's website (wholegrainconnection.org). Detailed instructions for making and maintaining a barm starter, making bread with that barm, lots of good recipes, plus much more. It is well worth spending the time. Monica Spiller is an enthusiastic advocate of whole-grain baking, and she really knows her stuff.

Recipe Index

Index

About the Author

VICTORIA REDHED MILLER grew up in Seattle and now lives with her husband, David, on an off-grid farm in northwest Washington State. She writes and speaks on a variety of sustainable-living topics, including food preservation, free-range poultry production, craft brewing and distilling, solar electric systems, and homestead repair skills. Victoria is also the author of *Pure Poultry* and the award-winning book *Craft Distilling: Making Liquor Legally at Home*.
www.victoriaredhedmiller.com

ABOUT NEW SOCIETY PUBLISHERS

New Society Publishers is an activist, solutions-oriented publisher focused on publishing books for a world of change. Our books offer tips, tools, and insights from leading experts in sustainable building, homesteading, climate change, environment, conscientious commerce, renewable energy, and more—positive solutions for troubled times.

We're proud to hold to the highest environmental and social standards of any publisher in North America. This is why some of our books might cost a little more. We think it's worth it!

- We print all our books in North America, never overseas.

- All our books are printed on 100% **post-consumer recycled paper**, processed chlorine-free, with low-VOC vegetable-based inks (since 2002).

- Our corporate structure is an innovative employee shareholder agreement, so we're one-third employee-owned (since 2015).

- We're carbon-neutral (since 2006).

- We're certified as a B Corporation (since 2016).

At New Society Publishers, we care deeply about *what* we publish—but also about *how* we do business.

Download our catalogue at https://newsociety.com/Our-Catalog, or for a printed copy please email info@newsocietypub.com or call 1-800-567-6772 ext 111.

New Society Publishers
ENVIRONMENTAL BENEFITS STATEMENT

For every 5,000 books printed, New Society saves the following resources:[1]

33	Trees
3,009	Pounds of Solid Waste
3,311	Gallons of Water
4,319	Kilowatt Hours of Electricity
5,471	Pounds of Greenhouse Gases
24	Pounds of HAPs, VOCs, and AOX Combined
8	Cubic Yards of Landfill Space

[1] Environmental benefits are calculated based on research done by the Environmental Defense Fund and other members of the Paper Task Force who study the environmental impacts of the paper industry.